RAISING
THE RESISTANCE

RAISING
THE RESISTANCE

A Mother's Guide to Practical Activism

FARRAH ALEXANDER

CORAL GABLES

Cover Design: Elina Diaz
Cover Photo/illustration: Angelina Bambina/stock.adobe
Layout & Design: Elina Diaz

For permission requests, please contact the publisher at:
Mango Publishing Group
2850 S Douglas Road, 2nd Floor
Coral Gables, FL 33134 USA
info@mango.bz

For special orders, quantity sales, course adoptions and corporate sales, please email the publisher at sales@mango.bz. For trade and wholesale sales, please contact Ingram Publisher Services at customer.service@ingramcontent.com or +1.800.509.4887.

Raising the Resistance: A Mother's Guide to Practical Activism

Library of Congress Cataloging-in-Publication number: 2020940773
ISBN: (print) 978-1-64250-374-6, (ebook) 978-1-64250-375-3
BISAC category code: FAM032000, FAMILY & RELATIONSHIPS / Parenting / Motherhood

Printed in the United States of America

Table of Contents

Introduction

At the dawn of the millennials—the 1980s—time traveling was all the rage. Marty McFly went back to the future and things got awkward with his mom. Bill and Ted took an excellent adventure and saved Ted from being forced into military school, which would *not* have been totally rad. The idea behind the films we couldn't get enough of was this: what if we could go back to the past and change our future?

We look to history to understand the past and how it relates to today. Our present lives are made up of choices made in the past. First Amendment rights were established; now I'm writing this book. I became pregnant, and now I have two children. I didn't do the laundry; now my kid's wearing pajamas at three in the afternoon. Actions, consequences. Cause, effect.

The idea of going back into the past to change the future is impossible. I know Keanu Reeves made it look so cool, and that's a bummer. You can't travel back into time and prevent a global tragedy like the Holocaust by handing Adolf Hitler a Snickers bar. The opportunity to make a small change in the past to affect our present is gone.

But the opportunity to affect change isn't gone. We know the past affects the present, so doesn't the present affect the future? If one person's small action in the past could make a huge impact on the future, what kind of action could we take to change the future?

When you look around, it seems like the world is on fire. (And if we don't accept climate change, the world might one day *literally* be on fire.) Americans are deeply divided. It turns out electing a reality TV show host as president of the United States may have been a poor choice. Our democracy is in decline. People are suffering. Fox News commentators can bait the president into declaring World War III via Twitter. We were hit with a plague and were constantly looking overhead for a swarm of locusts. We get breaking news alerts and just say, "Oh, what the hell now?" Things are bad.

Things are so bad; this is being recorded. These moments are being etched forever in the history books of the future. Our grandchildren will study this time and want to know where you were and what you were doing. What you do now will shape what that moment looks like. What do you want to be proud to say?

When you look back in history, do you see yourself as one of the good guys? Did you read Anne Frank's diary and think you would be the one breaking the law to save Jews from certain death in Auschwitz? Well, you don't have to wonder what you would do. What are you doing now? There are concentration camps keeping migrants hostage while they wait in asylum purgatory to hear if they get to stay or sent back to their home countries, where certain death awaits them. Did you read "Letter from a Birmingham Jail" and believe you would have marched alongside Dr. King and fight for civil rights? Well, Black Lives Matter exists because Black lives are being senselessly, callously taken, and the fight for their rights continues. There is an opportunity to affect change all around you.

Mothers are in a unique position to change the present to affect the future. The resistance against bigotry, misogyny, and injustice is largely being led by women, especially mothers. Activists are out there pushing strollers as they protest or registering voters with babies on their hips. We not only have the heart for activism, we are raising the future.

If we want to live in a world without the hatred and bigotry we see now, we need to teach our children about love and equality. What is so cool about being a mom and raising these little humans is that their world is whatever we make it. If we believe anything other than treating human beings with respect, dignity, and fairness is wrong, then we must teach them that so it becomes their truth. If we want to make the future a kinder, more just place for our children to grow old, we need to do everything in our power to make it so.

Whether it's managing your family's busy schedule between school assignments and extracurricular activities or excelling in your career and still helping with your kids' homework, moms get it done. Might as well throw in defeating bigotry and saving the world while we're at it.

In this book, you will be given the tools you need to discover, or further cultivate, your path in fighting for change through political activism. By using your time, your strengths, and your parenting, you can leave a serious impact on our world. Let this book be your guide to harnessing your power and turning your passion into action.

As mothers, we have plenty of problems, and I'll dive deep into them: the threat of infringement on our reproductive rights, lack of proper women's healthcare and self-care, inequality in the household, inequality in our communities, the Mommy Wars, and lack of representation in our political landscape, to name a few.

But I won't just leave you raging over the current state of affairs. I'll follow each issue with easy, accessible ways you can fight the problem. These solutions are sometimes as simple as correcting a well-meaning but misinformed family member about racial inequality. (Your racist comments will no longer be tolerated at Thanksgiving, Uncle Mike. Pass the mashed potatoes.) Sometimes they're more involved, such as running for political office yourself. Although they may differ in time commitment and difficulty, all the solutions are well within your reach and power. Being part of the solution will feel so much better than diving into a pint of Ben & Jerry's and rage-Tweeting. (I'm speaking from experience on that one.)

We have a problem. It's not going to fix itself any more than our children are going to teach themselves to use their manners and eat their vegetables. They need their mothers and so does the country right now. Let's raise the resistance today for a better tomorrow.

PART I

Choice

CHAPTER ONE

Don't Let the Patriarchy in Your Home

In the resistance against fascism, bigotry, xenophobia, and injustice rising in the United States, feminism has been at the core of this fight. We've long established that women's rights are human rights, but oppression against women lingers all around the world. One of the people who recognized the huge scope of this plight was Jimmy Carter.

Yes, Jimmy Carter. When you think of badass feminists, this former president and peanut farmer may have not immediately come to mind. But as an authority on human rights, his recognition of the oppression of women as a core issue exemplifies the gravity of how the patriarchy harms women everywhere.

A man of faith and conviction, Carter has focused much of his life's work on civil rights and how best to protect them. After decades of unparalleled access to the world and knowledge of how it works, he came to a conclusion on the number one abuse of human rights on earth—the abuse of women and girls.

To support this, he points to abuse based on religious belief—or, he believes, religious misinterpretation—that has led to women becoming victims of female genital mutilation, forced marriages, and honor killings. He addresses the exploitation of poor people and imprisonment. He speaks of human trafficking, sexual assault, lack of equal pay, and the added cruelties women of color face.

Carter understands that to do our part to repair the world, we must prioritize and change the way we treat women. The problems he addresses are not just issues women faced decades ago or overseas. They're happening right here, right now. But there's hope to create a better future for women, and mothers can lead the charge.

The wonderful (and overwhelming) responsibility you have as a parent is shaping your children's world. They have so many questions, and they need you to fill in the blanks for them, but your answers become their truth. Realizing that children are just sponges who will soak up whatever you teach them about the world is when my diabolical plan to repopulate the world with baby feminist change-makers started to take hold.

I mean, come on. You tell a kid a sparkly, winged fairy sneaks in their room at night to take their teeth while they're sleeping? They believe that. An altruistic bearded stranger in a red suit squeezes down the chimney every winter to leave gifts? They find that plausible. I don't think teaching them that men and women should be treated equally is that far-fetched in comparison.

Since the dumpster fire presidential election of 2016, we've been hit time and time again with events that have been incredibly unkind to women. Trudging forward when we keep getting pushed back feels daunting. I constantly hear dejected moms ask, "What now? What can I do?"

Just be a mom.

The progress you want to see in the world starts at home. You have the power to raise your children to be exactly the kind of people the world needs. Promoting gender equality, rejecting bigotry, and standing up for your beliefs can be your family values.

Kids don't simply mimic their parents when it comes to gender roles and politics. But the relationship children have with their parents and the way topics are introduced in the home comes into play. I can't guarantee your kid will never become a modern-day Alex P. Keaton sporting a MAGA hat, using Breitbart buzzwords, and grouching about an imaginary war against white men, but we can at least reduce that possibility.

Children are tiny adults in training with complex emotions, navigating their way around our great big world. They may buy your tooth fairy tales now, but soon they'll be independent and critical thinkers with their theories about how the world should work.

Political scientists Christopher Ojeda and Peter Hatemi studied the correlation between a parent's political leanings and their children's, once the children became young adults with established affiliations.

What they found is that the young adults were more likely to share the same political leanings as their parents if they had a healthy relationship and felt supported and connected to them. If they had a negative relationship and the parent was dismissive of the child's thoughts and feelings about politics, the child was more likely to reject their parent's views.

But nurturing a positive relationship with your children isn't just a self-serving exercise, so they'll one day share your beliefs about things like politics and gender equality. It's just good parenting!

Here are a few ways you can raise your children to be the patriarchy's worst nightmare:

Respect Kids

I know how maddening it can be to try to empathize with your child who is throwing a temper tantrum because you gave them the green and not the blue cup, but try to dig deep and muster up just a bit of empathy and understanding even in the most difficult circumstances. The ability to empathize with others, truly see them, and understand their struggles is fundamental to compassion. Compassion is often what fires our pull toward political activism, and we should practice compassion not only when engaging in activism, but in our homes with our children.

Validate their feelings. Try to avoid dismissing their feelings by saying, "you're ok" when they say they're hurt. Instead, help them identify what they're feeling, so you can help them appropriately. Listen when they tell you how they feel. Their feelings are very real to them, and it's important that they feel heard.

You don't have to play armchair psychologist and fully dissect their feelings. Just let them know you hear them and understand how they feel. A simple, "I know you're feeling sad right now, and I'm here for you" will suffice.

By opening up the lines of communication, you become a safe place for your child. If they're hurt, they know they can come to you, be heard, and feel comforted. This is especially important as they get older and need to ask someone difficult questions or confide in someone.

Tone down the baby talk. Your child is a much tinier and clumsier person than most people, but still a person. So try elevating your conversations and speak to your children much like you would anyone else. Use basic, natural vocabulary, and avoid the cutesy blabbering.

Imagine someone suddenly spoke to you in a much simpler, basic, juvenile manner than they did their peers. Well, assuming you're a grown woman reading this book, you've surely become well accustomed to mansplaining and do not need to imagine. You know it's terrible. It feels patronizing and disrespectful. By speaking to your children much like you would anyone else, your child sees that you respect them just as you would anyone else.

There's no magical age a child hits that suddenly deems them worthy of respect. Show them respect early and regularly. Soon, they'll view themselves worthy of respect, and when someone dares show them less than the respect they deserve, hopefully, they'll identify it as such and won't stand for that shit.

Children are too often the target of injustice, and as a society, we don't always treat them as compassionately as we should. Think about how difficult it must be to be a child. Maybe you remember how difficult it was at times and that experience still shapes your adult world. Kids live constantly under the rules of their parents and can't make their own decisions surrounding their own lives without permission. This is important because otherwise, kids would live on diets purely consisting of Captain Crunch and try daredevil stunts they see on YouTube. Parental rules are important, but they can be frustrating to a child.

Children are often treated harshly and don't have the same protections adults do. If someone strikes me, I can file assault charges against them. It's not just illegal, it's wrong. It's not ok to purposely hurt someone. This is one of the basic principles many of us teach our children—hands to yourself! But if I were to hit my child, that's legally sound. It's legal in all fifty states. There are more than five decades' worth of research that proves spanking children is harmful, but it's still practiced as if it's a valid form of punishment. Why would children, who are still developing and the most vulnerable among us, not be entitled to the same rights that adults are?

Spanking is one example of not respecting children. If you hit your children, you're not showing them compassion and you're causing harm, both immediate physical pain and long-term detrimental effects. But the most troubling thing about this idea and its widespread acceptance is that children are different and less than adults in some way. So, spanking is justified. That's not compassion. That's oppression. How can we possibly fight oppression in the world if we allow it in our homes? We must always exercise compassion for others and that includes showing it to our children mindfully.

Think Outside the Toy Box

Gender reveal parties during pregnancy are still are the rage, celebrating the baby's gender usually with stereotype-laden decor. Lashes or 'staches! Boots or bows! Pearls or Pistols! (Yes, unfortunately, that last one is real.)

Blue is for boys…or girls! Pink is for girls…or boys! Don't make it complicated. Try not to push your preconceived notion of gender on your child before they even enter this world. These expectations are just social constructs. In the 1800s, pink was viewed as a masculine color representing strength and reserved for little boys, and blue represented femininity and was mostly reserved for girls. But, regardless of gender, babies just wore white dresses because even in the nineteenth century, they knew they would have to bleach some stains because babies are messy as hell. Even science has proven that young children don't have color preferences based on their gender.

Frankly, I do understand the desire to dress your baby girls in frilly dresses and little boys in button-up shirts like little men. Newborn babies don't specifically look like boys or girls in the beginning. Most of them look like potatoes.

But open yourself up to the possibility of your child not embracing every little dream you had about having a son or daughter. Your daughter may not want to try ballet class, but your son may. Your son may not want to play football, but your daughter might. From the beginning, just try to follow their lead. Give them the freedom to discover what they enjoy. Allow your kids to play with a variety of toys without considering their sex. You may be surprised how they gravitate toward dolls and trucks regardless of their gender.

The reason behind gender-specific toys is often sexist. Why do little girls play house and rock dolls to sleep? So they can pretend to run a household and raise children. Well, doesn't it make just as much sense for little boys to play with dolls, pretending to one day be fathers?

Young children learn by playing, and research shows playing with different toys encourages different skills. Toys like puzzles and blocks encourage visual and spatial skills. Boys are generally more apt to play with these toys and develop stronger spatial skills. Toys like dolls and tea sets encourage social and communication skills. Girls are more apt to play with these toys, and their social skills are typically stronger than boys.

These skills are really important for young children to develop and have lasting effects. By limiting children to gender-specific toys, we're also limiting their chance to build a broad base of skills. So it turns out all those old, grouchy uncles who warned boys not to play with dolls because it would make them weird were wrong. Boys will be weird if they *don't* play with dolls.

It's most beneficial for all children, regardless of sex, to play with a variety of toys. Instead of being strong in only one set of skills, by playing with a variety of toys, they'll strengthen their spatial *and* social skills.

Kids get the idea that it's not ok to veer off from traditional gender roles from outside influences, especially through ads. One study published by the journal *Sex Roles* showed that when kids were shown gender-stereotypical ads, they were more prone to fall into those stereotypes.

The experiment went something like this: An ad is shown to a group of young girls. In the ad, a little girl says, "Hello! My favorite toy is My Little Pony." The little girls saw the ad, then were given a variety of toys to play with, and chose to play with the ponies just like the girl in the ad. A group of little boys was given a similar ad featuring a little boy who said, "Hello! My favorite toys are cars." Just like the test group of little girls, the boys also chose to play with cars after seeing the ad.

A different ad is shown to a new group of little girls, and this time, the girl in the ad says, "Hello! My favorite toys are cars." So what does the new group decide to play with? Cars. The same scenario with a new group of boys—faced with a new ad (now they see a boy playing with My Little Ponies) they pick up the ponies during playtime.

Between the commercials that pop up while our kids are binge-watching *Paw Patrol* (no judgment) and the messages we and their peers send, kids are getting ideas about what toys are appropriate for them to play with and which aren't, and it's heavily influencing their choices.

As parents (and major consumers of toys), we have the power to influence toy makers and retailers to knock off this silly gender stereotype shit. The parent-led grassroots organization, Let Toys Be Toys, calls for an end to gender-based toy segregation, and it's working. For example, major retailer Target announced they were no longer separating boy and girl toys, instead having one harmonious, gender-neutral toy section.

When it comes to toys, just follow your kid's lead and let them know it's ok for them to like what they like. It's perfectly fine for boys to play with blocks and trains while girls play with dolls and kitchens, but be sure to show them all the options available and allow them the freedom to choose for themselves.

Watch Your Language

Every time a parent excuses their son's behavior as boys being boys, they should have to throw a quarter in a jar and donate it to Planned Parenthood. We'd have them funded for decades. Pap smears for everyone!

I know it's easy to do. I would have thrown quite a few coins in myself. I've made an effort to give them freedom beyond typical gender norms, and my son and daughter have been extremely different in many ways. My daughter is adventurous, emotional, outgoing, and well…loud. My son is cautious, friendly, kind, and still loud, but he's never unleashed that banshee-like shriek that my daughter has mastered.

I've caught myself asking, "Is it because she's a girl? Is this a boy thing?" And I've caught myself falling right into those stereotypical compliments, fawning over my little princess and my handsome little guy. It's ok to slip sometimes and throw a few coins in the hypothetical jar. But it's important to be aware of what language we use when speaking to our kids regarding gender.

Be careful not to excuse misbehavior as being typical of boys. Boys are perfectly intelligent and capable of modifying their behavior. Stick to your house rules and enforce them. Don't enforce rules differently for children of different sexes. You got this! If your kid is in toddler tornado mode and destroying everything in sight, it's not because he's a boy. It's because he's being a little turd and kids can just be turds sometimes.

Likewise, don't let your daughters off the hook for stereotypical "girl" misbehavior. If your daughter is throwing a fit in the middle of Target and doing that crazy banshee scream, just run away. No, I'm kidding. But correct the behavior and maybe let her know it's not acceptable to scream uncontrollably in public.

Correcting these behaviors early and consistently not stereotyping any behavior as typical for girls or boys is key. Some people live their entire lives escaping the consequences of their actions and others accept this. When Donald Trump bragged about "grabbing women by the pussy" to correspondent Billy Bush before an *Access Hollywood* interview, enough people excused his behavior as "locker room talk" and just boys being boys (instead of a fifty-six-year-old man committing sexual assault) to elect him president of the United States.

As parents, we're constantly competing against these examples in the media for our children's attention. It seems harmless when our children are just fumbling toddlers, but when the behavior continues to be excused, it evolves like a misogynist mutant.

The public often encourages a sexist double standard that too often harms women and pardons men.

Women are stereotyped as being too emotional. So women chasing positions of authority have to balance being human and not exhibiting too much feeling. If the woman shows too little emotion, she's called shrill and cold. But of course, if she shows whatever is beyond the Goldilocks standard of the right amount of emotion, she's considered unstable and her emotional state a hindrance.

Take Hillary Clinton, for example. When she testified before the Senate after four Americans were killed in Benghazi through a coordinated attack, she calmly answered questions while being grilled by Republican senators (who care a lot about emails) for eleven hours.

Instead of being commended for her stamina and steadfastness in honestly answering difficult questions without becoming emotional or angry, she was criticized for not being emotional enough. Fox News commentator K.T. McFarland said the Benghazi hearings gave her a glimpse into Clinton's soul and it was (cue ominous music) "chilling." (McFarland was later appointed Deputy National Security Advisor for the Trump administration, a role that doesn't require Senate confirmation.)

When women do express emotions in understandably emotional circumstances, they're criticized as well. Dr. Christine Blasey Ford's voice cracked in an attempt to hold back tears as she described then Supreme Court nominee Brett Kavanaugh's alleged attempt to rape her when she was a teenager. Despite her testimony under oath and reputation as an esteemed scholar with much more to lose than to gain, she was dismissed by many as a liar whose emotions were insincere.

Men in similar situations have been considerably more emotional than Clinton and Blasey, but their behavior was not just tolerated, it was commended. After multiple women accused Supreme Court nominee Brett Kavanaugh of sexual misconduct, Kavanaugh testified before the Senate regarding the allegations. During the hearing, Kavanaugh wiped away tears, mocked senators, broke into angry outbursts, and mentioned how much he liked beer thirty times.

Kavanaugh was praised during the hearing by Republican senators like Lindsey Graham who called the hearing "hell" and continuously called Kavanaugh a good man who should not be destroyed by these allegations. Kavanaugh was confirmed to our nation's highest court shortly after the hearing.

Violent and toxic behavior is too often excused as being stereotypically masculine. When young boys are surrounded by the harmful stereotypes of boys being boys, toxic masculinity becomes what it means to be a man.

Although the term "toxic masculinity" is often dismissed as being radically feminist, the discussion began with men. Anti-sexism educator Jackson Katz spoke about violence against women during a TEDx talk and said although domestic violence and sexual abuse are often called "women's issues," they're intrinsically men's issues. Violent behaviors are tied to definitions of manhood, and according to Katz, we all need to be leaders of change against toxic masculinity.

Men are not naturally violent, and women are not naturally delicate. Research shows there's very little difference in the minds of little boys and girls. The behaviors they exhibit as either "girlish" or "boyish" are simply learned.

Sure, our kids get other societal influences from school, other friends or family members, TV, etc., but we as parents have tremendous influence in teaching our children what it means to be a girl or a boy.

So instead of gendering behavior, why don't we just teach our children how they should be regardless of their sex? Boys and girls can both be smart, strong, tenacious, and kind.

There's no excuse for both girls and boys not to be good humans.

Representation Matters

Children learn a lot of stereotypes at home and in the roles they see both men and women play. If a child never sees any type of diversity in certain industries, they'll grow to believe those industries are exclusive clubs for one gender.

Kids start thinking about what they'll be when they grow up very early. Four-year-olds typically have strong aspirations, but they also have a strong gender bias when it comes to thinking about jobs. Boys tend to lean toward occupations that are more stereotypically for men. (Firefighters! Police officers! Construction workers!) Girls usually lean toward occupations that stereotypically feature women. (Mothers! Teachers!

Nurses!) Fantasy is still a factor at that young age, so there's also a strong possibility they want to grow to be unicorns.

As the children grow older, they begin to look at future aspirations more realistically. The unicorn fantasy leaves, and sadly the gender bias tends to stick around. But it is possible to combat it and teach children they're capable of being exactly who they dream to be.

Overcoming the biggest obstacle in combating gender bias for our children's aspirations is quite easy—they just need to be told they can do it. Children often have rigid ideas of what men and women can become just because that's what they've seen, and they haven't been told otherwise. Research shows language can be a really powerful tool in showing young children that their aspirations shouldn't be restricted by gender.

Often, certain occupational descriptions default to a man occupying the position. So just be mindful of how you describe different occupations. For example, instead of saying "congressman," just say "congressperson" or "member of Congress." It's a very small linguistic difference, but it makes a big impact on small children.

As consumers, we have many choices about the people we hire and the people we expose our children to. Be mindful of the messages this sends to our children. If a child is only exposed to men when they go to doctor's appointments and contractors working on projects around the house, they may come to their assumptions that these fields are exclusively for men.

When children instead see both men and women in a variety of fields, they don't look at these fields under the lens of gender bias. When children see people like them represented in different careers, that promotes their interest and grows their confidence.

Think about the accomplishments that you have achieved even when it looked impossible. Did you break into a male-dominated field and dismantle the boys club? Were you the first female to hit a milestone? Have you experienced gender bias at some time when working toward a goal? Have these discussions with your children. Tell them about the obstacles you faced and how you broke through them. This will encourage them and show them how freaking cool their parent is.

Don't keep your badass female friends with incredible gender-defying careers a secret, either. Tell your kids about them. Encourage those friends to attend your kids' school career days. Talk to your kids about the glass ceilings they broke and how your kids can do the same.

There are countless female heroes in a variety of fields you can expose your children to just by incorporating some new titles in your child's library. Chelsea Clinton's *She Persisted* features thirteen American icons including Oprah Winfrey, Sonia Sotomayor, Sally Ride, and Harriet Tubman. Debbie Levy's *I Dissent* tells the story of America's Bubbe Ruth Bader Ginsburg and her affinity for disagreement, from standing against inequality as a lawyer to her famous dissents as a Supreme Court Justice. Elena Favilli and Francesca Cavallo's beautifully illustrated *Good Night Stories for Rebel Girls* showcases one hundred incredible women with a wide variety of careers including paleontologists, writers, rock stars, politicians, astrophysicists, and weightlifters.

If you keep telling your kids they can be anything they want to be and that you so fiercely believe in them, they're going to start believing you.

Enlist Your Kids in the Fight Against Inequality

As a millennial, I grew up with baby boomer parents who avoided divisive topics like politics. The first time I spoke to my parents about anything political was when I asked to put a John Kerry campaign sign in the front yard since I was still in high school and didn't have a yard of my own. I knew my parents always voted; in fact, my dad was usually one of the first to cast his ballot when he arrived at the polling place at six o'clock before starting his workday. But when it came to expressing their political opinions, that wasn't something they did. That's exactly what they first told me when I asked to put a campaign sign in their yard before they reluctantly allowed it.

I'm sure that by politely avoiding politics, my mom would have never been unfriended by as many people as I have been on Facebook, and she surely escaped some uncomfortable conversations. But I also believe the overall lack of conversations about politics and basic civil discourse has led to a lack of understanding. Americans are so fiercely divided and seem unable to grasp the nitty-gritty of politics and how different people approach the same issues in such different ways.

We can learn a lot from each other if we challenge ourselves to keep open minds and listen to other perspectives. We may never agree on an issue, but we can agree to respect each other and peacefully coexist. Giving your children some familiarity with political discourse will help them build those bridges later in life. When I was very young, my parents didn't talk about politics until I showed an interest. But as an adult, I have had the most enlightening conversations with both of them about how their personal experiences influence their positions and their feelings about the current political climate. My dad also regularly texts me some fresh political memes.

You don't have to save all topical or political conversation for after the kids are in bed. But you don't have to burden your kids with heavy topics like the military-industrial complex either. If it feels unnatural or your kids aren't receptive, don't force conversation. Just find a nice balance of discussing important topics in age-appropriate ways your kids can understand and relate to.

Your kid has probably already asked questions about your activism or feelings about certain topics. Like, what march are you going to? Why are you marching? What does that button mean? Why do you roll your eyes when Sean Hannity comes on the TV in a restaurant?

Unfortunately, you and your children will no doubt come across real-life examples of misogyny and bigotry. But by talking to your kids, you play a crucial role in shaping the narrative and how your kids view inequality.

Even children can play a role in combating inequality. In fact, I think they can play an especially crucial role as their innocence and optimism contrast so starkly with the ugliness of prejudice.

Long before she became Duchess of Sussex, an eleven-year-old Meghan Markle was disgusted by an Ivory soap commercial that declared "women all over America are fighting greasy pots and pans." She became even more enraged when she heard a couple of male classmates laugh in response and agree that women belong in the kitchen.

Even decades later, she still remembered feeling angry and hurt over the blatant sexism. When she confided in her dad about the issue, he encouraged her to write letters, so she wrote letters to the most powerful people her eleven-year-old self could think of—Gloria Allred, Hillary Clinton, and Nick News anchor Linda Ellerbee—in addition to the soap manufacturer Proctor & Gamble.

Ellerbee responded by sending the Nick News crew to interview Markle, which was pretty much the nineties kid equivalent of Anderson Cooper knocking on your door. In 1993, she told the Nick News crew simply, "I don't think it's right for kids to grow up thinking that mom does everything."

Proctor & Gamble responded by changing the commercial exactly in the way Markle suggested, removing the word "women" and instead just saying "people all over America are fighting greasy pots and pans."

All Markle had at the time was a little spare time to write letters, a few postage stamps, and the encouragement of her parents to challenge inequality, and she successfully changed a national ad campaign from a giant corporation, while calling attention to the issue of sexism.

Talk to your kids about inequality when it happens. Find the strength within yourself to discuss what exactly is happening and why it is unjust. Ask your kids questions about how it makes them feel. Then talk about how you can make a change, either on a micro level as Meghan Markle did as a child or on a larger level. Committing to confronting bigotry when it presents itself can be a lifelong journey as you fight for a more just world for all. Involving kids in the fight early is one way to help society work toward that goal.

Children themselves can be powerful agents of change. Malala Yousafzai was shot by the Taliban for pursuing education as a young girl and is now a student at Oxford and a Nobel Prize laureate. Eight-year-old Mari Copeny, a.k.a. "Little Miss Flint" met President Obama, called attention to the water crisis in Flint, Michigan, and has raised thousands of dollars to help her community. At only eleven years old, Naomi Wadler was the youngest speaker at the March for Our Lives and beautifully called for action against the epidemic of gun violence.

The most prolific champions of the climate change fight are the ones most affected—children. Greta Thunberg has worn her iconic yellow raincoat all over the world demanding action, and she was declared Time Magazine's Person of the Year due to her activism. Autumn Peltier has been an environmental activist since she was only eight years old. Autumn explained the sacredness of water in her indigenous culture at the United Nations as she lobbied for water conservation and access.

Your child doesn't have to be a Malala, a Mari, an Autumn, or a Naomi. But let them know they can be. Just because they're small does not mean they can't make a big impact. Help them realize their power to influence change. Give them the freedom and encouragement to blaze their own trails.

By raising our children to be advocates for change following the very simple, common-sense principle that all human beings are deserving of equality, our parenting can influence the next generation to reject bigotry and finally make strides toward equality that doesn't yet exist in our world.

With our help, our children can positively change the world. We just need to empower them to do it.

CHAPTER TWO

Our Bodies, Our Choice

Today I asked my body what she needed,
Which is a big deal
Considering my journey of
Not Really Asking That Much.
I thought she might need more water.
Or protein.
Or greens.
Or yoga.
Or supplements.
Or movement.
But as I stood in the shower
Reflecting on her stretch marks,
Her roundness where I would like flatness,
Her softness where I would like firmness,
All those conditioned wishes
That form a bundle of
Never-Quite-Right-Ness,
She whispered very gently:
Could you just love me like this?

–Hollie Holden

Love Yourself

As we tackle the fundamental human right of bodily autonomy, and before we get into reproductive choice, I think there is one crucial step we each must take—choosing to make peace with your own body.

No, I'm serious.

Now, first I want to recognize that promoting body positivity is not simple. I wish you could just seamlessly make the conscious choice to love yourself and your body. I wish it was as easy as cranking up Lizzo and bravely buying a crop top even if the label says, "plus-size." For some of you, maybe it is that easy. Maybe you not only have made peace with your body, but you love your body and enter every room with the confidence and beauty of a woman who knows her worth. And if that is you, I am so happy that you see the beauty in yourself that is so obvious to others, and I'm proud of the work you've done to get to this point. Keep being fabulous.

But for many of us, this is hard work. We look at our bodies, and maybe they remind us of a time of trauma, abuse, or assault when we didn't have control of our bodies. Maybe we look at our bodies in constant comparison to waifish models and live striving to attain a body type that doesn't even exist beyond the realm of Photoshop. Maybe when we see the stretch marks left as souvenirs from pregnancy, instead of empowered us, they just remind us that the bodies we've lived in our entire lives feel suddenly foreign.

We could lose ten pounds, one hundred pounds, but no diet or exercise plan is going to take away the weight of these issues revolving around our bodies. You can't measure that on a scale. We carry some heavy stuff, and it's not extra pounds.

I have some female friends who I'm fiercely proud to know.
They're the type of women who are doing incredible things,
have genuinely kind hearts, are always encouraging, celebrate
your successes, support you during your failures, and are like-
minded in all the ways that matter. Like all women—we're
busy! It's always hard to find time to see each other. But they're
the kind of people very much worth finding the time for
because they leave you feeling warm and inspired.

But too often we meet after trying to find time for months
and what do we talk about? Fucking diets. *Oh, I'm trying to
avoid carbs right now. No, it's not like Atkins, it's keto! Oh, I'm
counting calories. Do you have this app?* Enough!

Look, I don't want to hear about food unless you discovered
some amazing, new taco place and you are taking me there
to get tacos *right now*. I don't want to spend any more of our
precious time together talking about the magic of cauliflower
and how many carbs you can replace with it. I want to spend
our time talking about your brilliant ideas and what you think
about the world around you.

Now if you're doing something to improve your health, and it's
become a positive force in your life, fine, I want to hear about
that. I want to hear about how lifting weights makes you feel
strong and empowered. I want to hear about how skipping out
on booze makes your mind feel clearer and sharper.

But the conversations I hate are the ones where you talk about
how you hate your body. If a bystander said any of the mean
things I've heard friends say about *themselves*, I would say,
Hey! Cut that out. Don't talk about my friend like that. And
yet, women say terrible things about their own bodies all the
time, and instead of telling them they're beautiful and should

try being kinder to themselves, we join in and tell them all the things we hate about our bodies.

I say "we" because I recognize I've been a part of this problem. I was in second grade the first time I said I was on a diet. I was at a Girl Scout meeting and when offered a piece of cake, I politely declined explaining that I was on a diet. For some reason, I don't remember anyone being horrified that a nine-year-old just claimed she couldn't have cake because she was dieting. Instead, I think they just dismissed it as a child not fully understanding what she was saying. This was true, I wasn't actually "dieting" and didn't know what that meant. I was just imitating what I had seen grown women around me doing and I thought that's what women did—they diet and say no to cake.

I'm not going to tell you to eat the cake or don't eat the cake. You may be diabetic, you may embark on a diet for health reasons, and I am not a doctor. You absolutely should not take medical advice from me. I probably drink enough coffee in a day to fuel a lawnmower, and cheesecake is my love language. I respect you to make your own decisions regarding how you fuel your body.

The only thing I would suggest to you is to choose to love yourself and your body now. Don't wait to love yourself once you lose weight or get more toned or whatever your goal is. Love yourself now.

You are worthy of love right now, just as you are.

I understand that the work necessary to love yourself and accept your body, just as it is, can be incredibly difficult. Making a conscious effort to accepting your body may not be enough. You may need to dive deep into those issues that affect the way you feel about your body. Maybe you can't do it alone and you'll need a therapist. Maybe you'll need to practice positive self-affirmations. It may be hard work, but it is work worth doing because this is the body you possess, and your feelings about it often project far beyond Target's fitting room.

Now, you may be thinking, *what does this have to do with feminism and political activism?* I would argue a lot.

Self-love:

+ Is an expression of bodily autonomy.

+ Combats misogyny.

+ Helps you exercise better mental time management.

OK. Stick with me, here. Bodily autonomy is considered a fundamental human right. The gist is pretty simple—you govern your own body. It's the principle behind the "my body, my choice" rallying cry. This has been a crucial right for women historically. Bodily autonomy isn't something that is found explicitly in the United States Constitution, but the Supreme Court of the United States has ruled that there is an inherent right to privacy, which is alluded to in the fourth amendment. This right to privacy has been the basis for landmark cases giving women the right to obtain birth control without their husband's consent (Griswold v. Connecticut, 1965) and the right to obtain abortions (Roe v. Wade, 1973).

We fight for the right to control our bodies and govern our own bodies. These rights have been ardently defended by strong women throughout history and continue to be fought. We have the right to choose what to do with our bodies, so why should we choose to hate them?

In a world of diet culture, digital airbrushing that makes cellulite look mythical, catcalling, and general nastiness, loving your body is practically a radical act. As governor of your body, get radical, declare your bodily autonomy, and choose to love your body.

Secondly, the practice of hating women's bodies is deeply rooted in misogyny. Hurling insults against women, and in particular, attacking their bodies, is a misogynist's favorite pastime. Misogynists aren't notoriously clever, so they often rely on sexist jokes, sexual harassment, and childish verbal attacks.

Take Donald Trump. Trump has insulted dozens and dozens of women over the past thirty or so years of his hapless relevancy in the public eye. Some of the insults seem to be completely random attacks, as his obsession with *Twilight* actress Kristen Stewart and her relationship with costar Robert Pattinson. That's right, in 2008, the housing bubble popped, we suffered the most severe recession since the Great Depression, and what was a future president furiously tweeting away about?

A teenage actress of a sparkly vampire movie. Eleven times, a man in his sixties tweeted about Stewart's recent breakup and gave unsolicited relationship advice to her former flame.

Now, I don't personally know if Trump was an avid young-adult fantasy reader at the time or if he was just a big fan of the Twilight movie because Trump's attacks on women, even young women like Stewart at the time, seem to just pop up on Twitter or reported by media sources completely unprompted. He's attacked so many women at such a dizzying rate over such a long period, it's impossible to determine the method in the madness. He just attacks and insults women, especially regarding their appearance, openly and without discernment.

Like many misogynists, however, Trump is fairly predictable in one area. If a woman is smart, powerful, and publicly disagrees with him—sound the Twitter notifications. Trump will use his platform to attack these bold women with cheap, childish insults. He doesn't have the intellectual stamina to make an actual argument on the issues a strong woman is discussing. So he just calls her fat or ugly or whatever adjective of four letters or less that tickles his fancy.

Attacking a woman's appearance is classic misogynist behavior. It means absolutely nothing. You've probably heard of or seen this behavior when a "nice guy" begins to talk to a woman. The nice guy says hello, strikes up a conversation in which he claims he is a "nice guy" for no reason at all. The woman politely responds to the conversation. Nice guy makes a suggestion—*Want to go on a date? Maybe drinks? Maybe just come to my place?* The woman politely declines; she isn't interested. Nice guy calls woman fat. Or ugly. Or a slut. Or again, whatever insult of four letters or less that tickles his fancy.

This happens far beyond Tinder or the dating scene. If a woman discusses something in the public sphere that a misogynist disagrees with, he'll swoop in as if he heard Tucker Carlson light the misogynist jackass signal and alert all the misogynist jackasses that a feminist said something. The insults almost always revolve around appearances. Small minds are just not capable of sharp rebuttals, so they stick to the cheap shots. They'll attack your weight, face, what you wear, absolutely anything. Also, it has nothing to do with your actual physical appearance.

You are a beautiful, brave person with a voice that should be heard. But, when you do use your voice, be prepared for some misogynistic cretin to insult you and attack your appearance. Because misogynists, unfortunately, lurk among us.

Until that changes, you must remember the attack is a reflection of the misogynist's inward ugliness and has nothing to do with you. And remember, you love yourself. And why the hell wouldn't you? You exude beauty. You are brilliant. Your ideas are so powerful in fact that some sad sack is threatened by you and throwing cheap shots your way as if that would even bother you. Please. You're a goddess and you know it.

Misogynists throw these nasty insults because they want it to hurt. They don't value women; they think women are simple and shallow, so they insult appearances because they think it'll hurt the most. They think so little of women that they believe our top priority must be how attractive we look to them. They assume we are like fragile dolls so dependent on their opinions of us, they can break us with petty insults.

Show them they're wrong. Surround yourself with self-love like it's a big, fuzzy blanket. Don't give them an ounce of satisfaction. Don't allow their vile, meaningless words to hurt you. When you do this, the misogynists lose power. They lose the attention they crave. They lose any legitimacy. By simply choosing to love yourself and disregarding unworthy haters, you are actively combating misogyny.

And lastly, you should embrace self-love because you don't have time! I know you're already spending your time and mental energy in your career, in your relationships—women are overworked and tapped out.

Even though your time is a precious and fleeting commodity, you also have passions. You care about the world around you and are committed to doing your part to make it a better, more compassionate, and kind place for everyone. That is a very big undertaking. The work you do—whether it's volunteering for a cause you deeply about or getting people politically engaged— is vitally important and, because you are such a spectacular person, you are doing it!

But all the time you put into your passions and activism is a time commitment.

You'll have to manage your time and mental energy as you expand your commitment to political activism. We'll talk more about time management and self-care in a later chapter. But, for now, you just need to recognize that your time and mental space are valuable. Your time is too precious for one single second to be spent hating your body or yourself.

Wherever you are in the journey of choosing to love yourself, keep in mind this is a worthy endeavor. You will be you, in your body, for all of your days. Choosing to love yourself is an act of resistance to misogyny and should be the first choice you consciously make regarding bodily autonomy.

Respect and Love Other Women

In the endless abortion debate, reproductive rights activists often use heart-wrenching examples to prove that the right to choose must be upheld. We've all heard the stories of a mother making the impossible decision to terminate a much-wanted but terminal pregnancy due to extreme medical necessity, or the young woman who was raped and couldn't bear to carry a pregnancy caused by her rapist. These stories are often used to show that ok, yes, abortion is not ideal, but there are extreme circumstances that tug on the heartstrings of even hardcore abortion opponents like Senator Mitch McConnell[1] to get them to defeatedly admit, "Ok, ok, fine. *That* abortion is justified."

But here's the thing about the reasons a woman has an abortion—the reasons don't matter.

Now, sure, our heart-wrenching examples should be addressed, but not in terms of reproductive choice. If a woman is raped, impregnated, and chooses to have an abortion, the problem is that she was raped. Let's focus on preventing rape and supporting survivors as they heal. If a woman chooses to terminate a pregnancy due to extreme medical necessity, let's keep the focus on supporting the woman's extremely difficult decision and promoting proper prenatal care to keep everyone safe and healthy.

Remember, the constitutional backing for reproductive justice is a fundamental right to privacy. So while these emotional stories may compel people to agree that abortion is sometimes justified, justification is moot. There isn't a hierarchy of just and unjust abortions. A woman who was impregnated as a result of rape is not more entitled to abortion due to her circumstances than a woman with an ol' run-of-the-mill unplanned pregnancy. The circumstances are none of our business—anyone's business.

When the Supreme Court Justices debated Roe v. Wade, they did not decide what is a "just" abortion and what isn't. They ultimately decided that it was none of their damn business why or whether a woman chooses to have an abortion. And still, more than fifty years later, it is none of our damn business.

---

1   LOL. Just kidding, Mitch McConnell doesn't have a heart.

Of course, this courtesy should extend far beyond a woman's right to choose, even if that's an evergreen hot topic. We must respect women to make any and all decisions, especially about their own bodies.

There's so much toxicity around how we treat women and so much of this comes *from other women.* Too often, women help keep the patriarchy thriving by unknowingly perpetrating misogynistic behaviors in small ways. For example, we vote against our interests and against female candidates, rationalizing, "she's just not likable." We buy tabloids that show celebrities' cellulite and provide fabricated details of their personal lives, often sensationalizing abuse. We're just flat-out unkind to each other—we pry into each other's personal lives, we ask questions like when a woman is going to start a family, not considering that maybe she's been trying unsuccessfully for some time.

We judge other women for the decisions they make, and mothers are especially guilty of this. The sanctimonious moms (i.e. sanctimommies) judge every move you make from the moment that at-home-pregnancy-test turns blue. *Oh, you're drinking a cup of coffee, don't you know that has caffeine and is going to turn your baby into a rabid spider monkey? Oh, you're planning to have an epidural, are you sure you want to dull the pain of pushing a nine-pound baby out of your hoo-ha? Oh, you're sending your kid to public school, don't you know that's where they snort the marijuana?*

All of this is patriarchal bullshit that hurts women. When we're aiming to defeat misogyny and respecting ourselves and our own bodies, we need to lend the same respect to other women. If you actively work to love yourself, treat yourself with love and respect, and then treat all women around you with love and respect, your life will be richer for it. If more women took this same approach, imagine how different our world would be as we're liberated from the silliness that hurts all of us and holds us down.

I know that in our society, these steps can feel like a wildly radical act. But, get radical! Love yourself, love other women, and let's reclaim our bodies and ourselves from these ridiculous patriarchal narratives.

Respect the Choices of Other Women

As a mother, you're faced with many, many (too many) choices to make. If you're carrying a baby, you must decide everything from whether to drink caffeine to if you'll find out the sex of the baby to what kind of birth you'd like to have. If you're an adoptive parent, you may choose whether you want an open or closed adoption or if you'll pursue domestic or international adoption. No parent is immune from making tough decisions about how they'll parent. Then, once the kid is earth-side within your family, you have a myriad of choices to make while you navigate the mind-blowing notion of having a new little human under your care.

You'll choose whether to breast or formula feed, to work outside the home or stay at home, and how to discipline your child. The one constant is that, no matter what you choose, someone will hoist on their judgy pants, ready to tell you how wrong you are.

Women and mothers are badasses. We intensely care, love, and want what's best for our babies. Sometimes we don't innately know what's best, so we research and learn more until we've found the perfect fit for our families. And we feel pretty good about our decisions!

And then another mother faces the same decision and approaches it with care and love with the same goal of choosing the best option for their family. But she chooses something different.

Instead of two mothers recognizing that, first of all, motherhood is really freaking hard and it's no easy task to make these decisions, or that they're both coming from the same place of love and wanting what's best for their children—they flail around arguing why their decision is best and why mothers making opposite decisions are just wrong, wrong, wrong.

This absurd phenomenon is known as the "Mommy Wars" and it's detrimental not only to mothers but to women and feminism in general. Just explaining it to you now makes me feel dumber for it. But we must discuss it because you will kill many more brain cells if you enlist yourself in it.

Take breastfeeding, a fiery hot topic for Mommy War soldiers. In general, the phrase "breast is best" is considered the gospel truth. In reality, breast may or may not be best, and it's a highly individual choice.

For many mothers, breast is not best. It's probably not best for a breast cancer survivor who had a double mastectomy. It may not be best for a sexual assault survivor with certain triggers. It may not be best for a mother who needs to treat her postpartum depression with a medication that isn't compatible with breastfeeding. It may not be best for a mother who just doesn't want to. And *none* of these mothers owe explanations to anyone.

Formula isn't poison, and the child just needs to be fed. Although there are some benefits to breastfeeding in general, they're often overstated. I doubt even the most zealous breastfeeding advocate would be able to pick out which kids in a kindergarten classroom were breastfed and which were formula-fed.

Often, the topics that divide mothers the most deal with issues of bodily autonomy—infant feeding, pain management during labor and delivery, when and if to have children at all, and so on. A mother's body does not cease to be her own just because she can carry, birth, and nourish a child.

What's so silly about this dynamic of mothers judging and shaming one another is that not only does it hurt women, like most forms of misogyny—it's pointless. No mother gets a trophy for enduring unmedicated childbirth, and no mother is more of a mother than another. Neither mothers nor their children benefit from Judgy McJudgerson supermom criticizing their parenting. The truth is, none of these battles matter. In several short years, all your kids will be hopelessly weird and eating chicken nuggets they rescued from between the couch cushions.

So, refuse to participate in the Mommy Wars. Another mother's choices are not an attack on your choices. Parenting is damn hard, and it serves none of us to make it harder by judging another mother's choices.

The only caveat to this is if the mother or child is in *danger*. If a child appears to be in some type of danger, by all means, intervene. But first, approach compassionately. If you're concerned a child isn't being adequately fed or isn't in an appropriate car seat, consider why that could be. Is it possible the mother is living in poverty? If so, prepare community resources and approach the mother with love.

Always approach other mothers with empathy. No one's path is like your own. Don't make blanket judgments about anything. For example, I am strongly pro-immunization. Stick my kids with all those glorious vaccines. No polio or measles over here. And yes, I'll take a flu shot, please, and thanks. But I cannot and will not make any blanket judgments about mothers who choose not to vaccinate, because there are always legitimate exceptions. A child with leukemia who is undergoing chemotherapy and as a result is immunocompromised, typically cannot receive vaccines. Now, I think this is a good case for why everyone healthy enough for vaccines *should* get them and do their part to contribute to herd immunity. But I digress. The point is that even when you think you there's a one-size-fits-all method to some aspect of parenting, there may be some factor you're not considering, and it turns out your method isn't the only way. Ever.

It's best to just get rid of the judgy pants. Don't even put them back in your closet or stowed under your bed. Burn 'em so you're not tempted to slide them back on.

Intersectionality Is a Must

When I first heard that there would be a march in Washington, DC, shortly after Trump's inauguration, largely to protest the misogyny and bigotry that got him elected in the first place, I was freaking *in*. I booked a ticket to ride a bus with a few friends and my mother from our small town, where the majority is white and Republican. We drove twelve hours, straight overnight in a cramped bus, went to the march, and then hopped right back in that damn bus to drive twelve hours back home.

When we returned, I faced many people who were disgusted that I participated in the march. I lost many Facebook friends, including ones with whom I share a last name. I was shunned from certain local mom groups. Things got awkward.

When you live in a town in which more than 60 percent of the people voted for Trump, you're going to know some Trump supporters. You're going to be in the minority. These people are all around you—they're your neighbors, your kids' teachers, maybe even your siblings or your parents. I couldn't escape, so for the ones who opted out of blocking or shunning me, something in me just really wanted to tell them about the march, why I participated, and how great it was—I was desperate to reach them in some small way.

So instead of talking about the platform or exactly why I, or anyone, marched that day, I chose to talk about how peaceful it was—how I took place in the largest single-day protest in the history of the United States and it was completely peaceful. Not a single person was arrested! Heck, when I saw police officers, they smiled at me and I even got a high-five!

How. Very. Foolish. Of. Me.

Yes, the march was peaceful. No, no one was arrested. But why didn't I immediately notice that the vast majority of the participants looked just like me?

After the District Attorney's office in Sacramento, California, announced they would not be filing charges against the police officers who killed Stephon Clark, a peaceful protest was organized. Clark was a twenty-two-year-old Black man who was killed in the backyard of his grandmother's house after two officers mistook the cell phone in his hand for a weapon. The crowd of demonstrators was mostly Black and included members of the clergy and residents of the affluent neighborhood where the protest took place. Eighty-four people were arrested.

If you're a white woman like me, this probably doesn't give you the warm fuzzies. It probably feels uncomfortable, a bit icky. But we need to have these uncomfortable conversations. We don't deserve to feel the warm fuzzies when we recognize that the privilege and power we possess has historically come at the expense of marginalized communities.

I have a chapter dedicated to unpacking privilege later in this book, but when I talk about "women," I want to be as clear as a circa 1992 Crystal Pepsi—I mean *all women*. Whether you're participating in a march or you fought for a seat at a table in a room where decisions are being made—look around and make damn sure not everyone around you looks like me. When you're discussing issues that affect women, make sure you're not only considering women who look like me. When you surround yourself with like-minded women who want to make a difference and combat bigotry and misogyny, make sure they don't all look like me.

I want you to consider everyone who identifies as a woman across the spectrum. I want you to consider women who identify as LGBTQ, impoverished women, undocumented migrants, immigrant women, religious and secular women, incarcerated women, disabled women, minority women, indigenous women—*all* women.

To be truly compassionate, you have to look beyond the lens of your own experience and fight for the rights of others. None of us are free if others are still oppressed, and we cannot deny that oppression is not happening.

Take virtually any issue that negatively impacts women in general and it likely disproportionately affects marginalized women more so. For example, the #MeToo movement revolutionized how we view sexual misconduct and for perhaps the first time, really showed the scope of sexual harassment and assault that women have endured. But women in marginalized communities are more likely to become victims of sexual assault. Due to systemic racism and a whole host of other reasons, they're less likely to be believed. (And even rich, white, Ivy League-educated ladies like Christine Blasey Ford widely aren't believed, so…that's pretty bad.)

For example, almost 19 percent of white women have experienced rape. 22 percent of Black women, 27 percent of Native American women, and 33 percent of multi-racial women have been raped. Nearly half (47 percent) of transgender women have been sexually assaulted. And migrant women? Well, who the hell knows because they often avoid reporting for fear of detention or deportation, and many instances of sexual assault happen in immigration detention.

When we're discussing these issues, we need to ensure every woman's voice is heard, and we always need to be mindful of their perspectives. Never look at an issue that affects women and think only about how it may affect you personally, or women like you. Instead, explore how the issue affects marginalized women, and make sure you're fighting for them too.

I use the term "marginalized" because I want to be inclusive of all women, and I want to be clear that I'm not talking about cis white women in heteronormative relationships like myself.

This term works best in my opinion because it includes women of color, the LGBTQ community, impoverished women, incarcerated women, migrant women, and essentially any group of women facing a heightened amount of inequality.

To marginalize means to put someone in a powerless position within society. When you marginalize someone, you're pushing them to the edge of society, and I'd like you to keep that idea in mind when you think about inequality. Many of the issues we fight for are because we, as women, feel marginalized in some way. We're being pushed out of the process that governs our lives. But I want you to be mindful of the marginalized communities who are being pushed even further away. When we're fighting for our places within society, far from the margins, make sure we're bringing everyone with us.

Do Not Apologize

Your choices are your own. You've made your choices to the best of your ability with all the information you had available. The decisions you've made are highly personal, and someone else in the same position may not have made the same choices, but that doesn't mean they're wrong.

You are a smart, capable, worthy person, and you should be trusted to make your own decisions regarding your body and your life because no one is better suited than you to make those decisions.

If it empowers you to share your story and your experiences, then feel free to do that. You should be met with only support and love. But your story is yours to share, and if it compromises your security or mental health, then your decision *not* to share is completely valid.

You never owe anyone an explanation just to satisfy their curiosity. You do not need to constantly justify or apologize for your choices. Be bold and stand strong in your convictions. As we're fighting for equality and combating misogyny, we don't have time to apologize for choices that don't warrant apologies. We deserve respect. We will show respect to each other. We will command respect for ourselves.

CHAPTER THREE

Their Bodies, Their Choices

I walked along with my mother, a couple of my closest friends, and millions of our fellow discontented feminists in the inaugural Women's March past the Beaux-Arts style Old Post Office near the White House. The Old Post Office stands out both in its stature and beauty among the rest in DC—it's gorgeous. It served as the local post office until the beginning of World War I. But now, it's just another Trump hotel complete with the signature, gawdy brass letters in front—"TRUMP."

As we approached the building near the rally point, people ditched their signs in front of the building. The entrance of the gorgeous building tainted by the vulgarity of the Trump name was soon covered by signs that said, "Girls just want to have FUNdamental rights," "My Body, My Choice," "Hate Won't Make America Great," and quite literally thousands of others.

The building looked beautiful again.

A young mother walked nearby with her toddler nestled close on her chest in a baby carrier. My mom, being my mom and someone who always has an iPhone no further than hip-distance away, asked the babywearing mother if she could take her photo. The mother smiled politely and said, "Sure!"

My mom fumbled with her iPhone and just as she raised it to take a pic, the toddler scrunched her nose and shook her head. After all, it was a chilly day near the end of a march with millions of people. Can't blame a toddler for not feeling camera-ready. So, the mother sweetly smiled, kissed her toddler's head, and said, "Ok. Your body, your choice." And told my mom, sorry, no photo after all.

During a day of historic moments, this simple thirty-second exchange still stands out because a mother honoring her child's bodily autonomy felt both sensible and yet somehow radical.

As parents, we control what our children do, wear, eat, and much of the way they live their lives. And generally, that's fine because otherwise those little gremlins would survive solely on Lucky Charm marshmallows and watch a continuous loop of YouTube until their little brains were thoroughly washed. And it's permissible to take complete liberty in choosing your infant's outfit and plans for the day because…they're a baby. I assume they're too focused on keeping their big ol' wobbly head upright than to have opinions about their outfit. Other than the cycle of eating and pooping, having a newborn is a bit like carrying a delicate sack of potatoes around. So, sure, if you want to treat your child as a bona fide accessory, that's the time to dress them as silly as you want.

But, soon, the babies get bigger and they start having opinions with what they want to do with their bodies and, as long as it's not harmful, (i.e., perhaps no stunts), their wishes should be respected. We must teach our children as soon as possible that they have rights to their bodies.

It's vital to set the precedent early that our children's bodies belong to them and they have rights. Allowing our children to express bodily autonomy early often leads to some slightly awkward social faux pas. You may need to ignore the side-eye glances from other parents as you drop off your daughter wearing a Queen Elsa dress and a pair of rain boots on a sunny day. Or you may find yourself explaining to Great Uncle Harold that your toddler won't be kissing him goodbye because, well, he doesn't want to and that's ok.

These moments of brief awkwardness will be worth the lessons you're teaching your kids about how you hear them and respect their wishes.

One of our ultimate goals as parents is to prepare our kids to live their lives without us. We teach them manners and to be kind, so they don't grow into little assholes. We may throw some money in their college savings accounts and help give them the tools to pursue higher education. We teach them to look both ways before crossing a street.

Teaching bodily autonomy is just another way we're protecting our kids and preparing them for the future. Sending our kids to college is this classic rite of passage—we imagine unloading boxes from our minivans, decorating their dorms, and how we'll try to squeeze in an extra-long hug before we wave goodbye and drive away. But, if you've considered this scenario, have you also considered that one in five female undergrads experience sexual assault?

I know I'm harshing your mellow, and the thought of incorporating some form of sex education into parenting a toddler is uncomfortable, but we *have* to talk about this. Many of us understand the horrific reality of being sexually assaulted in college because we survived it. We know we don't want that to be a college experience for our kids. So, what can we do?

Well, we can empower our children by proactively teaching them that they have ultimate control over their bodies and that it is not ok for anyone to take that control away. Likewise, everyone controls their own body, and it is not ok for them to take that control away from anyone else. I know this sounds daunting, but you have the power and you can do this!

Consent Is Mandatory, Always

Incorporating consent into parenting our kids is a super important concept and holy crap, are most of us terrible at it. The truth is, it's not easy and, especially if this is a new concept for you, you will slip up a lot. That is ok! Show yourself some grace and accept that slipping up is normal, learn from it, and try to do better next time. Focus on progress over perfection. That's all any of us can do.

The reason this is so difficult is that when your children were younger, you as the parent had to do nearly everything for your child. Hell, when they were infants they couldn't even do anything! You had to do everything from holding up their wobbly heads to wiping their bums to feeding them. And even now, you probably do a lot for them. They're terrible at washing and wearing socks, I get it.

So, a lot of incorporating consent is difficult because it may feel a bit unnatural and you as a functioning adult are generally more skilled than your children, so you'd rather take control. Of course! You naturally kick ass at almost everything, and everyone else pales in comparison. So it makes total sense to just take control.

But, as unnatural and mildly inconvenient as this may be, it really is important. By enforcing some really basic measures, you're teaching your children that they, and they alone, should have control over their bodies. When you're consistent, if anyone ever approaches their body without this respect given, they should recognize that this is not ok. Whether they're in elementary school or college, if nonconsensual contact happens, alarm bells should be going off in their heads that something is very wrong.

When you're finding the practice tiresome, keep this goal in mind. You're teaching your children that when they are touched:

+ They understand why.

+ They have given permission.

+ They are comfortable with it.

That's it. So every time you touch your child, make sure these criteria are met first. What this looks like in practice may feel a little odd. But the more you explore it, the more, I think, it will make perfect sense.

If you're bathing your child, just briefly ask if it's ok that you wash them. This exchange will take mere seconds, I promise it won't be a big chunk of your day. If they give you the green light, go ahead with the scrubbing. If they say no (and this is an option!), explain that they will need to do it themselves then and allow them to, giving verbal instructions as needed.

Use this basic practice and apply it to going to the bathroom, getting dressed, and essentially any time they may need assistance and it involves you touching their body. Relinquish the control over their bodies and transfer it to them.

My husband is a psychotherapist and has taught our kids lots of little quips some people grasp only after years of therapy.

Sometimes I ask my kids to do something not so fun like clean their rooms, and they'll calmly decline. Then when I *insist*, they respond with something like, "You're not the boss of me, Mom. You're only the boss of yourself and I am the boss of myself." It's empowering and completely maddening. It's like arguing with a two-foot-tall Brené Brown.

You may have identified this issue as you were reading about practicing consent with your child. How do we respect our children's autonomy and enforce responsibility? The way I approach this with my kids is to explain that yes, you are the boss of yourself and, as the boss of yourself, you have a responsibility to take care of yourself.

I keep in mind I'm trying to raise future autonomous adults, so I often relate to my own experiences and speak to them candidly. I explain that there are also things I don't want or like to do, but I must do them to take the best care of myself. There are consequences to my actions or inactions. I don't like to clean the house, but there are consequences if I don't. The dust would aggravate my allergies and the TJ Maxx bags would pile up so much, someone would nominate me for that *Hoarders* TV show. Consequences!

I make it clear that they have choices in terms of consent. If they don't want to be touched, they won't be touched. When it comes to bathing, for example, having their mom scrub them in the bathtub is optional. But baths are not. To be a responsible person, you have to practice good hygiene and bathe yourself. The choice they have is if they want to do it themselves, not give up baths and become mud people. I understand it can feel like an odd, unnatural practice. But try not to make it more complicated than need be. Just make it clear that their body is their own and no one may touch it without their consent, not even you.

I'm a super affectionate mama and I just want to smooch chubby little cheeks all day. But now I just ask first. Super simple—"May I give you a kiss?" "May I have a hug?" Most of the time, I get the green light. If I don't, that's the end of the conversation and I don't take it personally. Sometimes I want to cuddle with my husband, sometimes I want to lie alone like a starfish in bed. Sometimes I want to lie on the couch with a pile of kids on me, and sometimes I am just touched out. I get it.

This also applies to other people. Affection should not be expected or forced. I know it's commonplace during family visits to order the little ones to hug and kiss goodbye. Well, all apologies to Uncle Harold, but we have to put a kibosh on this. Affection is not mandatory; consent is. So, instead of ordering the kids to hug and kiss goodbye, ask them if they want to. If they decline (which is *fine*), ask if they'd like to blow a kiss or wave goodbye instead. Still no? Still ok.

This isn't at all weird compared to the bizarro-world where we force children to kiss people they don't want to. I certainly wouldn't want to be forced to kiss or hug someone, and I wouldn't tolerate that happening to any other adult.

Our children are just tiny humans. They have feelings and opinions just like we all do. They're not props or accessories and they don't solely exist to fulfill our wishes. We need to consider what message it sends to our children when we disregard their feelings and make demands about what they do with their bodies and how they give affection. Then, what message will they carry into their teenage years and adulthood?

They're constantly learning. We need to be mindful that we're teaching them the right lessons about consent, and that the message that they carry into their later years is that they—and they alone—control their bodies.

Boundaries!

I found myself quietly trying to take a peaceful poop one day when I saw the doorknob click and then turn. Oh, I had locked the door, of course. But my toddler had quickly discovered how to unlock the knob from the outside in less than thirty seconds. So, I clenched my knees together, threw my hands up, and said, "Hey! Mommy's using the potty here." But I was met with, "I just wanted to hug you. Can I have a snack? Are ya poopin'?" and finally, as she made herself comfortable in the corner of the half-bath, she told me reassuringly, "I'll just be right here if you need me."

Boundaries. Kids suck with boundaries.

As we talked about sexual misconduct and consent, you probably (and accurately) picked up that these practices help your children navigate what is and is not appropriate touch and affection. So hopefully, as our children get older and start exploring romantic relationships, they'll be able to recognize what is and isn't healthy in a relationship and draw a hard line that their consent is always mandatory.

But we also need to make sure our children don't grow to one day cross those lines. Most often, boundaries are carefully and subtly crossed. The "Stranger Danger" stories blasted on *20/20* of teenage girls getting kidnapped by middle-aged men driving vans are not the stories most women who experienced sexual misconduct live with. Instead, the stories women share are usually stories about men who are not strangers violating their boundaries, often from within the bounds of an existing relationship.

We sometimes catch moments in the public eye when a celebrity is exposed as a sexual predator. The Harvey Weinsteins of the world are well aware of their methodic evil. But often, before the celebrity launches a damage control PR campaign, you catch a genuine moment of astonishment, and I always consider, *Wow. Did they not realize that was wrong?*

Of course, it's wrong. You don't need to assault dozens of women like Weinstein for it to be considered wrong. If you harass or touch someone without their consent, it's wrong. Period. It's not a difficult concept, and yet, we have countless men among us dumbfounded that they had been playing a game with the wrong set of rules this entire time.

We have to get it right with the next generation and stop this cycle of clueless men violating women and feigning ignorance that they didn't know it was wrong. One simple way we can do this is to teach our kids about boundaries. These little bath time lessons about when it's ok for someone to touch their bodies are necessary for establishing their boundaries as well as respecting others.

I worked at a big-box hardware store as a young undergrad, and the harassment from customers was rampant. They didn't include how to deal with this behavior in any of the training videos, so we all found our own way. Personally, when someone invaded my space, I reached into my apron and pulled out my store-issued tape measure. Without saying a word, I stretched the tape out to three feet, placed it in front of me, and spun in a circle. I rarely had to say a word. They got the message that this was my personal space, and they were invading it. Sometimes they looked embarrassed and sheepishly backed away, sometimes they stomped away grumbling about my sub-par customer service skills. But either way, they got the message and went away, so goal achieved!

You don't need to literally measure the boundary of your personal space. You know where it is, and you know when it's violated. Even though kids are habitual boundary-invading offenders, they also tend to grasp this concept pretty easily.

In practice, you just encourage your children to show others the same respect you show *them*. When you're consistently practicing consent with your children, that will be the norm for your kids. They'll understand that before someone is touched, they need to give consent just like *they* give consent before being touched.

Allow your children to have some expectations of personal space and privacy. You don't invade their space unless they've given their ok, and they cannot invade others' space without the ok. Everyone has boundaries, physical or emotional, and it's not ok to cross them.

Although, again, boundaries are something that most adults have struggled with from time to time. Children somehow seem to grasp this fairly easily. Most schools have basic, universal rules they enforce such as, "keep your hands to yourself" and "treat others as you would want to be treated." Well, boundaries are a similar concept. Between my two kids, my preschool-age daughter is the one quick to shout, "Boundaries!" when her older brother gets too close.

When discussing boundaries with your kids, also discuss how it's ok to say "no." No is always an option, and it's a complete answer. If your kid is looking adorable and having a total

Instagrammable moment, you ask to take their photo, and they say no? No Instagrammable moment. You're not the paparazzi and they're not a Kardashian. (*Unless you are!! Kim—is that you?!*) If they're having a sleepover with a friend, but for some reason feel uncomfortable and want to come home, let them know that's fine and bring them home. If you want a kiss, but they're not in the mood, let it go.

Sometimes I don't know how we got here, but we're the grown-ups and we have the bills and lower backaches to prove it. When your child tells you "no" regarding something that crosses their boundaries, immediately accept that as a complete answer. Under no circumstances do you manipulate. Absolutely no pouty faces or "please?" pleading. No means no, period. We want our children to understand that when they grow up, so let's teach them while they're small.

Your children should also have some expectation of privacy. As long as you don't suspect your child is in some kind of danger, allow them to have their privacy. If they have a diary, don't sneak in and try to read it. If they don't want to share every detail of their school day, don't press. Explain to them that you always need to know if something is wrong, if they've felt unsafe, or if someone crossed their boundaries and made them feel icky, and that you are a safe haven that they can always confide in. But also explain that you will respect their boundaries and privacy.

As your children learn to identify their boundaries and to respect the boundaries of everyone else, you're setting them up to be able to one day identify and pursue healthy relationships while being good partners themselves.

The Freedom to Mix Patterns and Other Atrocities of Fashion

For children, self-expression is extremely important. This is something I typically take for granted as I wear the same Old Navy jeggings I've had since 2012 and my daughter refuses to wear the precious Mini Boden outfits in her closet. For me, my outfit choice is more often than not based on my preference for elastic pants (postpartum is forever, right?) and whatever else I remembered to wash and hang back in my closet. But many kids consider what they wear a form of self-expression they tend to take pretty seriously.

It may seem like a small thing. But when you look around your home and consider your child's environment from their perspective, you'll probably realize they may feel like they don't have many choices. The refrigerator and pantry are full of food their parents bought, and dinner is seldom the Fruity Pebbles and ice cream as they want. The decor of the home is more Joanna Gaines and less Pee Wee's Playhouse. They live in a world where most of the choices are made by other people.

Now, this is fair. They don't have many choices. We all have seen *Big* and *Home Alone*, right? When kids are left to make all their own choices, they make *terrible* ones.

But allowing them to make their own terrible decisions builds their self-confidence and assurance! Choosing what they wear is one easy way they can make their own choices and express themselves without any harm other than perhaps committing mild crimes of fashion. The worst thing that could happen is that they choose something a bit mismatched or silly, but big deal. Everyone will adjust.

Some kids may not have strong opinions about what they wear. My son would rather just have his clothes chosen if he can't have his first choice of not wearing clothes at all. My daughter, on the other hand, has strong opinions and will gasp and look as appalled as Jonathan Van Ness if I pick something she doesn't like. So, just follow their lead.

Even if they don't voice strong opinions as small children about how they dress their bodies, this may change when they hit their teenage years. Again, just take the same approach of following their lead and giving them a little freedom. If they want to put a little funky color in their hair or go for a super trendy cut? Meh! Go for it. It's just hair. Instead of trying to police their style, try to acknowledge their bravery and individuality. If the worst thing your teenager wants to do is put a purple streak through their hair, holy moly, you've hit the teenage years lottery.

You can use your judgment regarding what is "appropriate" and what isn't, of course. But I urge caution in discussing what is appropriate. Consider whether a literal or unspoken dress code applies equally to both sexes, whether you find it fair, and if you can easily rationalize it in a way that makes sense to both you and a child. For example, it could be as simple as explaining a wedding or religious holiday is a special occasion and you want to dress a bit fancier because it's a fancy day!

Some dress codes get sexist quickly. We're going to discuss that more in the next chapter. But in general, if you start to tell your child they can't wear the clothes they've chosen because they're not appropriate, ask yourself why you find them inappropriate. If there's even a hint of misogyny in your reasoning, stop.

Allowing your child to choose will probably mean much more to your child than it does to you. If they're wearing actual clothes and you've successfully gotten them out of the house (and maybe even on time!), does it *really* matter that they're not wearing what you would choose for them? Now think about how they might feel about it. They're probably thinking:

+ *Wow. I look amazing.*

+ *I chose this sparkly tutu and my favorite rain boots myself and I love them.*

+ *I did it all by myself.*

+ *If I plant the sesame seeds from my hamburger bun in the garden, will it grow hamburgers?*

The contribution to their self-esteem and freedom of expression is worth a side-eye from Karen in the carpool lane.

Healthy Body Image Starts at Home

Hating your body is a damn near-universal experience for a woman. Without knowing you, I still know that you have probably had negative thoughts about your body at one time. Also, you probably want to lose weight.

How do I know this? Because almost every woman has felt or feels the same way! *Psychology Today* conducted a study about body image, finding that most women are generally dissatisfied with their appearance. The severity of the study's findings was bat-shit crazy. An overwhelming 89 percent of women specifically want to lose weight. 15 percent of women even said they would give up five or more years of their lives to achieve their ideal weight. Women among us would literally choose death just to fit in some skinny jeans. What the hell!

It's such a universal experience that a woman may fantasize about looking like Chrissy Teigen and even though Chrissy objectively looks like a goddess, she too has struggled with the same dissatisfaction with her body! Women are stuck in this terrible loop of hating our bodies at times while wishing we had the bodies of women who also hate their bodies at times.

So, it's a pretty safe bet to assume you have an intimate understanding of body image issues and you acknowledge what an awful, limiting force it can be. While we actively work to heal personally, we also need to promote a healthy body image at home and keep our children out of this toxic cycle of negative body image.

Always be aware that your children are learning about body image from what you do and say. If you choose a salad instead of a burger, they might ask why. So, be mindful of how you respond and be honest. You can say salads make your belly feel better than burgers do, you're trying to get more vegetables, you just really like salads, anything! Just do not say you need to lose ten pounds, you're on an iceberg-only diet, or that you're "fat."

UGH. Fat. Fat may just be my least favorite "f-word." Some women call themselves fat in a disparaging way (which I *really* hate), some use it as an insult to others, and some call themselves fat to extract the power from the word and instead empower themselves.

Whether or not you feel comfortable using it, I think we can all do our part to take the power away from the word when we talk to our kids. Fat is a macronutrient and gives us energy. It's in a lot of the food we eat and isn't even necessarily bad for our bodies. We need fat. There is healthy fat like the fat in avocados! We all have fat in our bodies, some more than others. That's all fat really is. It doesn't define a person or tell us anything about who someone is. Everyone is so much more than the amount of a nutrient they carry in their bodies.

When your kids use the word fat, just refer to these basic facts about fat. We all have fat. We need fat. It's just a nutrient. The more you describe fat as a completely boring fact of life, in your kids' heads your voice will probably start to sound like Charlie Brown's teacher like it does when you talk about preventing cavities. That's fine. It *is* boring. That's a great attitude to have when it comes to fat. Then, they hopefully won't give much power to such a boring thing as they navigate their relationships with their bodies.

You should always be kind to yourself and your body for *you*. But if you're not motivated enough by treating yourself with the love and respect you deserve, do it for your kids. Don't be unkind to yourself or your body in front of your kids.

Don't jump into unhealthy fad diets. If you wouldn't be comfortable with your kid eating the same diet as you are, reevaluate. If you want a cookie, eat the cookie! Don't make a big production of it. You're not a puppy—don't say you deserve a treat or you're being "bad." Find a balance of healthy eating habits you feel good about and would be comfortable with your kids because they are learning directly from you in real-time.

Always be mindful of what you say about others' bodies. It's never cool to body shame. No matter how much you want to know about Jennifer Aniston's love life, if a tabloid has body-shaming bullshit on its cover, don't bring it home. Don't comment on other's bodies, especially negatively, in front of your kids.

This is a hard line. Body-shaming is never ok. So, because Donald Trump is a pile of human garbage, is it ok to poke fun at the size of his ass in tennis shorts? Nope. Think about what message that sends to other women and your children when you disparage someone for their weight. *Oh, that's what she feels. That's what she thinks. Is that what she thinks about me? Is that what she thinks about anyone of a certain size?* You want to criticize him, criticize his policies, and leave his ass out of it.

And of course, body-shaming is not ok for anyone of any size or ability. It's not ok to criticize someone for being too thin, or disabled, or having a different body. Body-shaming, in general, is not ok, ever. That's it. That's the message to teach your kids.

If someone has worked hard on a weight loss goal and you want to commend them, go ahead! But do it *carefully*. Don't disparage their previous body and say they look great *now*. Keep it positive—say things like, "You've always been beautiful," "You look so healthy!" "I'll bet you feel great," or "I hope you're proud of yourself for taking charge of your health."

Always be kind to your body. Your kids are learning how to have a relationship with their bodies from you. If you're unkind to your body, frown in the mirror as you pinch the fat on your midsection and complain about your weight, that is how children learn you feel about your body and probably how they should feel about theirs.

But it is not too late to turn it around. Stop being so mean to the only body you'll ever have. It can't be that bad. It's gotten you this far, hasn't it? Think about all the incredible things your body has done for you...all the places you've gone, all you've seen, all you've endured, all you've survived, all you've accomplished. It's amazing! Show your kids that a body does not have to be "perfect" (whatever that even means) to be loved.

It took me thirty-two years to learn that a bikini body is just a body wearing a bikini. I never felt comfortable enough to wear a bikini because I never had what I thought was the body type required to wear one. Even as a teenager, I was curvy and didn't look like the tall, thin girls wearing string bikinis in the Delia's catalogs I got in the mail. So I thought that bikinis weren't for me. The most revealing suit I had even worn was a "tankini," which is technically a two-piece swimsuit that might reveal a centimeter of midsection if you raise your arms to hit a beach ball. And always black! Black is slimming, of course, so no other swimsuit color could ever do.

At thirty-two, I was getting ready for a kid-free Las Vegas trip with my husband. I needed a swimsuit and gravitated to the familiar rack of black one-pieces with attached skirts and lots of ruching to conceal any midsection roundness. After birthing two babies and undergoing a couple of surgeries, my tummy looks like a battlefield of stretch marks and scars. Not to mention, my body type post-baby-birthing was different, and I carried much more weight with me now.

But, I thought, what the hell? If not now, when? If not fifteen years and fifty pounds ago, why not now? So I ventured into the uncharted territory of my local Target—the bikinis. And guess what? They had my size! Can you believe it? All this time I thought to wear a bikini, you must have a bikini body of a certain size. But nope. Sure enough, they had a variety of sizes all along.

I tried it on. My fluffy thighs and scars were on full display under bright fluorescent lighting. It didn't look anything like the bikini bodies I had seen in ads and magazines, but it was my body in a bikini. I liked it.

I purchased it subtly in a self-checkout lane. The purchase went fine. No error message saying, "Mayday! XL bikini bottom error! Do not sell!" popped on the screen.

Then, I actually freaking wore it. No swimsuit coverup. No oversized T-shirt. I just wore it to a hotel pool. And you'll never believe what happened next…

Nothing. Absolutely nothing. I sat on my chair. I read a book. No one seemed to notice or care that I was wearing a bikini for the first time in my whole damn life except me.

Part of the reason I decided to personally focus on body acceptance is the same reason I have the stretch marks—my stinkin' kids. I don't want them to remember me sitting on the side, covering my imperfections, and trying to become invisible. I want them to see me splashing in the pool and looking comfortable in my own skin. They probably *will* notice that my body doesn't look like a magazine cover. I hope they do. I want them to know that their mama has a bikini body, too.

CHAPTER FOUR

Stop Sexualizing Children, Creeps

I know you're familiar with this scene: two mothers with children of different sexes are having a play date. The children do what children do: they play, they pout, they touch germy things on the floor, stuff like that. Meanwhile, the mothers gush about how sweet their little darlings are together and then, as mothers do, assume they'll one day be joined in holy matrimony. And of course, they laugh and insist they're joking. But you know Karen already has a secret Pinterest wedding board and has been pinning away her favorite Mason jar centerpieces.

Put down the taffeta and stop planning your toddler's wedding, Karen. It's creepy.

I've heard so many parents of children who are kindergarten age and even younger discuss the children's romantic futures. They refer to their future dating lives and how popular their little gentlemen will be with the ladies or how their daughters are destined to break all the boys' hearts. And as I look over the crowd of kids who seem to care much more about pizza Lunchables than the opposite sex, I always have the same thought...

Some of these kids are gay.

I mean, say we're looking at a kindergarten classroom of thirty kids. (Overcrowding in schools, a real problem, I know.) If roughly 5 to 10 percent of people are gay, then probably anywhere from one to three kids in the classroom are gay. So, why are we assuming each one of them is a cis heterosexual?

It may seem like a small thing, but assuming a child's gender and sexual identity before they've established it themselves can be confusing and worrisome for kids if your assumptions are incorrect. For many, part of coming out as LGBTQ+ is telling those they care about that their heteronormative preconceived notions about them are wrong.

We tend to make a lot of stereotypical expectations of our children's futures regarding their sexual and gender identity when, truthfully, we don't know. We form many of these expectations when they are at an early age and don't even know. We need to give our kids the freedom to explore their own identities and the acceptance so that they know we'll love them endlessly no matter what.

So, look. If you haven't thought about this before and your child is young enough that *they* have not established how they identity, I need to tell you: your child might be LGBTQ+. Go ahead and consider this possibility now. Get cozy with the possibility even knowing they may be, and probably are, straight. Just be aware of the possibilities and consider how you'll incorporate this into your parenting.

The way you can incorporate this is pretty easy and is also the case for virtually all aspects of parenting: assume nothing. Don't assume your child is cis and straight. Be open to the possibility that they're LGBTQ+. The side effect of this if they turn out to be straight is that they have an early education of

LGBTQ+ identities and are hopefully less likely to be bigoted turds, so win-win!

Kids typically see adult relationships and ask questions. This is your time to shine. They know nothing. When you describe marriage, they respond that they're going to marry you or Daddy. Sound familiar? The idea of loving someone beyond their immediate family and wanting to spend all their time with that someone is quite bizarre.

So, when you discuss romantic relationships, marriage, things of that nature—keep it open. Instead of telling your son one day he'll find a woman to love or he'll have a wife, just say someone or specify man *or* woman. Then follow their lead. If it's brand new information they need to process, they might ask for clarification, "Oh, two boys can get married?" Then you can confirm.

This is also a good way to make sure they're not getting any harmful messages from outside sources. If they respond that Mrs. McBoomer-Frumpy Pants said two boys can't get married or with some cootie conspiracy theory, you can correct them and let them know that no, same-sex relationships happen and are completely loving, normal, legal, and lovely.

Think about what a gift it is to your children to teach them early that no matter who they grow to love, you'll accept them with open arms and hearts. This acceptance and love are contagious, and if it turns out your child is as hetero as they come, they will show the LGBTQ+ community they come across in their lives the same love and acceptance they learned from their parents.

Down with Discriminatory Dress Codes

I understand dress codes have a place in society because people are uncomfortable with others wearing pajamas or their birthday suits to the office and formal occasions. Also, I'll admit I am not comfortable with any student wearing clothing with truly offensive messages, such as hate speech, on them. I get it. Fine. Dress codes have a place.

What I am not fine with is sexist dress codes. I trust that you know the type—dress codes that exclusively and unfairly affect girls. You may have seen them on Facebook when frustrated parents show photos of their disappointed daughters in the offending outfit (often something that exposes a shoulder, or— *clutches pearls*—two inches of thigh) and shares a story about how they were sent home from school or turned away from the prom due to their accidental dress code violation.

The language in these dress codes unfairly targets girls by focusing on clothing that is most often worn by girls: tank tops, leggings, and skirts, for example. The message behind these restrictions is sometimes literally in the written dress code, described by an authority figure such as a school principal, or unspoken yet understood—these clothing styles are banned because they can pose a distraction to the male students and teachers.

Eww.

Think about what a horribly disturbing message this sends to young girls. Girls as young as elementary school age are being taught that their bodies are so inherently distracting to males, including the ones who are responsible for their education, that they must cover their still-developing bodies to avoid interfering with the educational experience of boys and men.

How distracting it must be for a girl to halt her educational experience so she can borrow a pair of sweatpants to wear instead and return to the classroom. She has to deal with the anxiety and fear that she's done something wrong and is in trouble. She has to leave the classroom while teaching moves forward without her, and she is forced to fall behind and try to catch up when she returns while not allowing herself to be too distracted by the embarrassment of having to change her clothes. Whose experience is more distracting in that scenario, the girl experiencing this enforcement of a silly, sexist dress code or the boy sitting beside her who may have caught a glimpse of a shoulder?

Then, most disturbingly, think about the message this sends to girls that their bodies are so inherently sexual that if what they wear exposes their body, they may distract the *adult males* in the school. How could a child possibly feel safe in an environment where the male teachers view her as a sexual object?

Distractions exist. You can dress a young girl in a potato sack and someone who has an interest in her will still find her distracting. Birds chirp outside. Students tap their shoes on the tile floor. Sometimes students bring outside stressors into the classroom, slamming their books on desks. It's impossible to ban all distractions from the classroom (unless you want to murder a bunch of noisy birds).

If you're concerned about distractions in the classroom, focus on things that hamper everyone's learning. Is the school in such poor shape that there's black mold and students are experiencing respiratory problems? Hmm, that sounds distracting. Do the students have enough time to complete their homework on top of extracurricular activities? Is the teacher too exhausted to teach because she was working late at her second job the night before?

These are all issues that are no doubt distracting and could probably be remediated by investing more funding into public schools, paying teachers a livable salary, and not overworking our kids. So, if you're concerned about preventable distractions, the list to tackle is long.

But the existence of girls is not a preventable distraction. If your child is so distracted by the appearance of a girl, then the best way to approach that issue is to teach your child coping mechanisms. The problem is not that a girl is wearing leggings, it's that the boy is so distracted by this, he's allowing it to interfere with his education. By far, the best way to approach this scenario is to teach the boy to cope with the appearance of girls so his head doesn't explode in the mall at the sight of a Victoria's Secret ad.

By the way, I'm calling bullshit on this whole scenario. I suspect this only exists in the imagination of adults inspired by their own sexism. Imagine this: little Johnny is sweating his way through a test, then the bell rings and, defeated, he turns in a blank exam. With tears in his eyes, he tells his teacher, "I think I would have performed better if I weren't so distracted by…the spaghetti straps." His male teacher grasps his hand and responds, "I know." They sob together.

That bad fiction stands on the same shaky ground that justifies these sexist dress codes.

The problem is not the existence of girls and their preference for the latest styles, which may expose a small bit of knee or shoulder. The problem is that we're teaching young girls that boys' education is so much more important than theirs that we're willing to sacrifice their education just in case they may pose a distraction.

This is the bottom line: if a girl's appearance is distracting a boy from his educational experience, he needs to work on his focus. If a girl's appearance is distracting a teacher from teaching his students, he should not be around children.

It wasn't difficult to figure out that dress code language involving short skirts, leggings, yoga pants, and the like are targeting girls. So, let me quiz you on this completely real dress language taken from a school. Guess who this targets:

> All boys' hair must be a tapered cut, off the collar and ears. There are to be no dreads, mohawks, designs, unnatural color, or unnatural designs. No combs or net caps.

Did you guess Black kids? *Ding, ding, ding!* In this specific case, a private Christian school enforced this policy. A sweet little Black six-year-old named Clinton Jr. arrived at school with his uniform polo and locs, which his parents permitted after Clinton requested them because he admired his godfather's locs. When Clinton Jr. and his father arrived at school on the first day, they were confronted with school administrators who told them Clinton Jr. would not be allowed to attend school due to his hairstyle.

Several times, Clinton Jr.'s father suggested holding his short locs back in a ponytail to comply with the dress code, but he was denied, and little Clinton Jr. was banned from school. Clinton Jr.'s parents quickly enrolled him in a public school in order not to disrupt their child's education further. According to the complaint, the child being banned from school gave Clinton Jr. quite a bit of emotional distress as you can imagine. His father fears he'll now feel shame about his natural hairstyle and, as a six-year-old, this incident has prompted tough conversations about race.

Everything about these policies is racist. There is nothing wrong or unprofessional about natural Black hairstyles. But these policies promote the stigma that Black hair is a problem. There are many, many dress code policies policing Black hairstyles with language banning, "dreadlocks, afros beyond one inch in height, box braids, afro puffs, hair extensions, or similar hairstyles."

Not only do the school administrators often not see their policies as racist, but they are also completely unaware of the racism in the very language they use. Here's a not-so-fun fact you may not know: there is a derogatory implication to the term "dreadlocks." The texture of Black hair naturally "locs." So, during the Middle Passage, English slave traders referred to their hair loccing as "dreadful." So these boneheads in school administration are not only making discriminatory dress code policies, it has an added layer of ignorance and racism by not knowing the history of the terms or the natural state of Black hair.

Hair loccing is a natural process and, by banning the style, schools are directly discriminating against Black children and interfering with their education. This ban is not directed at white kids because white kids have no business putting their hair in locs, but alas, that is a cultural appropriation discussion for another day.

The language used in these racist dress codes is just a more flowery way to attempt to ban Black hair. For example, "afro puffs" are just natural hair held back with elastics. If you're white, they might look like pigtails. If you're Black, they might look like afro puffs. If you're white, no one notices or cares if you wear your hair down or in a ponytail. If you're Black, your hairstyle may be a violation of a school dress code. Make sense? Of course it doesn't.

If a young, Black girl has natural hair that has never been chemically treated and it's pulled back, it may resemble "afro puffs." Many young girls like to wear their hair up and away, so it doesn't fall into their faces while they're coloring and playing. But by doing what every young girl and grown women with more than shoulder-length hair prefer to do, they're violating a dress code. How could they comply with the dress code? Would it be acceptable if a young Black girl chemically straightened her hair so it more closely resembles the hair of her white peers? Thaaaaaaaaaaat's racist.

We know that dress codes have a place and generally should exist. But we also know that the language in some dress codes directly discriminates, usually against girls and Black children, and that is not ok.

The problem is that we have tolerated discriminatory dress code policies for far too long when they never should have been tolerated at all. Now is the time to change that, and *you* have that power.

Take a few minutes and look at your child's school dress code. It may even be online on the school's website. If not, locate a student handbook if you were given one; it may be in there. Or if all else fails, go directly to the school and request a written copy of the dress code if they have one.

Now, read the dress code *critically*. If you see language that discriminates against a group of people, any group of people, or specifically polices the styles of girls or students of color, it's time to intervene or—as I like to say—cause a stink. At this moment, I want you to mourn the fact that you may be ruining your chances at a future PTO presidency and some moms might give you the stink eye. It's ok. You probably didn't want to participate in that many damned bake sales anyway.

Go directly to the principal of the school and challenge these discriminatory practices. Be cordial and polite, but also firm and direct. Be bold and confident—you know what you're doing. Back up your opposition to these policies with facts; show the principal news stories that tell the fallout of similar policies and the children they hurt. Some of these policies are in direct violation of the antidiscrimination provisions of Title VI of the Civil Rights Act of 1964 and certain state laws. Find the text of the law, cite it, and tell them they may be in violation. Use this language. They will pay attention.

After you've stated your case, end the conversation or correspondence with an ask—will you please revise your dress code and remove the discriminatory portion? See what happens. If you don't have any luck, time to move up the ladder and cause a stink at the next school board meeting. Repeat the process.

You can continue this process or escalate as you see fit. If you're not getting anywhere and the policies do appear to violate the law, consider contacting your local ACLU chapter. Find some new like-minded parent friends who also are alarmed by the discriminatory policies and would like to help. (Even better, now you and your new, smaller group of way cooler parent friends don't have to share your brownies.) Contact local news organizations about the issue; perhaps they could cover you and your new friends causing a stink at a school board meeting or speak to the parents of students of color affected by these policies.

Here's the harsh truth, when you take on these battles, you don't always win. This specific battle may be initially lost or won very slowly. However, if you do nothing and no other parent speaks up against this, the battle most definitely will be lost. Quiet parents have allowed these policies to exist. So, get loud. Tell them in no uncertain terms that this is not k and it does not help children. Keep fighting!

Sex Education

"Don't have sex, because you will get pregnant and die! Don't have sex in the missionary position, don't have sex standing up, just don't do it, ok, promise? Ok, now everybody take some rubbers."

–Coach Carr, *Mean Girls*

Ah, sex ed. A rite of passage for many awkward youths made so much more awkward by the absolutely mortifying experience of seeing your gray-haired gym teacher place a condom on a banana.

Adults sometimes swap horror stories from their days in sex ed…stories about trying to avoid seeing the countless graphic slides of STD complications, signing abstinence pacts, and enduring creepy lectures about how girls must remain pure for their future husbands or whatever other patriarchal garbage teachers spewed at the end of the twentieth century. But the real horror is that sex ed today IS STILL AWFUL.

I know we like to shield our kids from the existence of sex and allow them to believe for as long as possible that they were magically dropped into our arms by storks. But, one day, most likely, our kids will have sex. I know, I know. Stop grimacing.

They may be in high school. They may be in college. They may be married; they may not be. But one day, it is going to happen. They may never use the quadratic formula again, but they're likely going to have sex, and we need to consider what kind of education we want them to have as they navigate their sexuality.

The age-old "solution" to this educational quandary is simply to tell adolescents...DON'T HAVE SEX. This suggestion is more officially known as abstinence-only sex education. Abstinence-only sex education is just as it sounds, sex education that tells students, DON'T HAVE SEX. It's the easy answer to all questions teens may have about sex...

"How do I avoid getting pregnant?"

"Don't have sex."

"How do I avoid getting an STD?"

"Don't have sex."

"How do I, as a member of the LGBTQ+ community avoid STDs?"

Don't have...wait, a member of the what? That's not in the booklet. Just...don't have sex.

In addition to giving kids, who are inevitably going to have sex, the advice not to have sex, abstinence-only sex education often excludes the topic of consent and accurate information about birth control, promotes myths and fearmongering tactics regarding abortion and STDs, ignores the LGBTQ+ community, and uses religion and/or morality to shame kids about their sexuality.

Now, I'm sure this is not a shocker to you, smart reader, but perhaps the biggest problem with abstinence-only sex education is that it is completely and utterly ineffective. Evidence shows that it does not decrease sexual activity, unplanned pregnancy, or the spread of STDs. The only thing it succeeds in is making people feel guilty and wholly ill-prepared when they do decide to have sex.

You know those toothpaste commercials that tout those ridiculous statements like, "Nine of out ten dentists agree— brushing your teeth is important." And you're just thinking, *Ok. But what the hell is up with that tenth dentist? Where did they find that guy?*

Well, abstinence-only sex education is recognized as an awful, ineffective program that should be used by absolutely no one, pretty much across the board. The American Academy of Pediatrics, the American School Public Health Association, the American College of Obstetricians and Gynecologists, public health researchers, and psychologists all say abstinence-only sex education is absolute garbage and they support comprehensive sex education instead.

But just like that tenth dentist, some people support abstinence-only sex education knowing how ineffective it is, and often these people are loud and wield a great deal of power.

Remarkably, the United States has spent approximately two billion dollars (billion with a "b") on abstinence-only sex education. This is remarkable because abstinence-only sex education has not just been proven completely and utterly ineffective and useless, it stigmatizes all adolescents (but mostly young girls), completely ignores the needs of the LGBTQ+ community, and often provides incorrect information.

The fact is that 95 percent of Americans decide to have sex before they're married, and, on average, begin having sex around age seventeen. The abstinence-only approach of having the school gym teacher shame teens into not having sex is not working. 95 percent of teens need accurate information or they're otherwise having sex thinking that condoms cause cancer because that's what they learned in abstinence-only sex ed.

President Obama and members of his administration did something really outrageous and revolutionary concerning abstinence-only sex education—they looked at the facts, which clearly show that abstinence-only is only effective in putting adolescents at a greater risk of contracting STIs and having unplanned pregnancies. Then Obama proposed in his 2017 budget to cut federal funding for abstinence-only sex education.

But, of course, the budget cuts were just one more action of Obama's that Trump vowed to reverse.

Obama's proposed cut to abstinence-only education was (no surprise) not executed, and instead, the Trump administration proposed an *increase* in abstinence-only sex education. Congress allocated eighty-five million dollars to abstinence-only sex education in 2017. So, the proposed amount allocated to abstinence-only sex education was zero dollars, and the actual amount was eighty-five million.

Abstinence-only sex education is still so prevalent in the US that there's a good chance your child's school still teaches a version of it. You need to take charge of your child's sex education or the only education they'll get will be like that Coach Carr scene in *Mean Girls*, but not as funny.

Do your best to cast aside your uncomfortable feelings about your child one day having sex. Properly educating them about and preparing them for sex does not make them have sex earlier than they would otherwise. Again, they will most likely have sex one day. By educating them, you're giving them the necessary tools to be safe and have a healthy sex life...one day.

When we accept that our kids being forty-year-old virgins is unlikely, we need to also think about what we want for our children regarding sexuality and relationships. Maybe even consider what *you* wished you learned in sex ed or what you would have benefited from knowing before you started having sex.

Just talk to your kid. Talk about what a healthy relationship looks like—being kind, having mutual respect for each other, having boundaries and privacy, having fun together! Talk about what toxic signs to look for in a partner that are unhealthy—a partner making demands, being constantly critical, controlling, isolating from friends and family. Make sure your child knows to look for the strong red flags like emotional or physical abuse, coercion, or any type of nonconsensual acts. But it's important to also let them know that those strong red flags are not the only benchmarks of a bad relationship.

If the relationship doesn't feel good or they just want to break it off for any reason, they should be free to do so, and that is completely ok. They must know that they deserve a healthy, happy relationship that makes them feel good and they shouldn't accept anything less.

Also, teach them about teaching others with the same respect they expect for themselves. Be kind and respectful, don't make demands, don't try to control, be a good listener, and be honest about your feelings.

Stress to them that on both sides, consent is *mandatory*. It is never ok to touch someone without their explicit permission, nor is it ok to be touched, forced, or coerced either within or outside the bounds of a relationship. In most acts of sexual misconduct, the predator is known to the victim, so it's important to tell your children that being in a relationship is not consent. Only consent is consent.

No need to give them nightmares about gonorrhea, but just let them know that there are risks associated with sex. The one accurate pearl of wisdom the abstinence-only sex education model teaches is that abstinence is the only 100 percent foolproof way to prevent unplanned pregnancies and STDs. Emphasize the safest ways to minimize risk while sexually active, such as by using more than one form of contraceptive simultaneously, like a birth control pill and condoms.

Let them know about the options available to prevent STDs and pregnancy. Again, no need to scare them straight with episiotomy horror stories. Just be honest. By some cruel twist of fate, teenage girls are super fertile. If you both feel comfortable, talk about the birth control options available. If you don't feel so comfortable, the Planned Parenthood website is a valuable resource for evidence-based contraception information. Be mindful of your child's privacy. If you take your daughter to the OB/GYN and birth control may be discussed, let your daughter know you can give her time to discuss options with the doctor without you hovering in the corner.

Don't let birth control solely be a girl's responsibility. Have the same conversation about the same options as your sons. Give your sons equal privacy and opportunity to access reliable birth control methods. Give them the facts and tips they may not know, such as the fact that you should not store condoms in your wallet.

If your child identifies as LGBTQ+, be sure and address their individual needs. All the same advice about healthy relationships and consent apply. Be careful not to stigmatize them or share outdated information, such as that they're at particular risk for contracting HIV. If you think an in-person learning opportunity would be best, there are many wonderful LGBTQ+ organizations with local chapters, and many of them focus on adolescents. My personal favorite LGBTQ+ organization is the local chapter of the Sisters of Perpetual Indulgence, the Derby City Sisters. The Sisters don't focus solely on adolescents, but they are an active charity involved in the community and in advocating safe sex. If anyone would know where to turn for comprehensive sex education for your LGBTQ+ child in your community, they would.

Sexuality is going to be a part of your child's life, and when you think about it and accept this simple fact, don't you *want* it to be positive? If they're going to enter romantic relationships, don't you *want* them to be healthy ones? If they're going to be physically affectionate, don't you *want* to make sure it's consensual? If they're going to be sexually active, don't you *want* them to be safe? Of course you do! Getting over your hang-ups about having awkward discussions and ensuring they have a proper sexual education is how you set them up for a healthy future in their sexuality and relationships.

Although it can be a frightening time for parents and adolescents alike, it's also a vital time to establish healthy relationships and understand how to be safe. You may shudder to think of your children one day having sex, but I have no doubt you want them to be prepared for when they do.

Girls Have Value Beyond Their Hymens

On a podcast, a well-known rapper felt compelled to share strange, intimate, and possibly medically inaccurate details about his eighteen-year-old daughter's hymen. That's right—her hymen. He said he accompanies his daughter to the gynecologist annually and "has her hymen checked" to ensure she is still a virgin. Typically, around the time of her birthday, as she's taking inventory of her gifts, he leaves her a note reminding her of their arrangement that simply and ominously says, "Gyno. Tomorrow. 9:30." (Not even a "Happy Birthday!") Then, to really drive the creepy, possessive father role home, he proudly proclaimed, "I will say, as of her eighteenth birthday, her hymen is still intact."

So, there are many, many problems with this. Rightfully there was a great deal of public backlash toward this reported hymen monitoring. On a technical note, a hymen is not a sign of sexual experience or inexperience. It's possible to have sex without breaking a hymen, and it's possible to break a hymen without having sex. Attending your daughter's gynecologist appointment *to check on her hymen* is a classic what-not-to-do example; it violates all the biggies: bodily autonomy, privacy, accurate sexual education, and generally not being a controlling, creepy parent.

But the example also touches on the importance of virginity. Like many parents who put great emphasis on the importance of maintaining virginity, this specific rapper and others only emphasize virginity with their daughters, not their sons, which is deeply sexist and misogynistic.

Virginity really means…nothing. It's just a social construct. In other words, we made it up. It's not a medical condition. It's not a state of being. It doesn't change who someone is or isn't. It's just the concept of describing someone who has not yet had sex. To make things even more complicated, what does that mean? Is that strictly penis in vagina penetration, or does oral sex also count as losing virginity? Is a lesbian who never had penis in vagina sex a lifelong virgin? Does any of this make sense? (No.)

The concept of virginity tends to have special importance among certain religious and/or cultural groups. Virginity is often linked to a girl's worth, value, and honor. This is where the bullshit meter starts buzzing. A girl's worth is so much more than virginity! Her life has tremendous value beyond whether or not she chooses to be sexually active. But the virginity concept has infected churches, social groups, and schools with things like virginity pledges and purity balls and shame young girls for daring to have sexuality beyond what someone else chooses for them.

I have no doubt you've either personally grappled with the concept of virginity and what it means for you or you recall a girl who did. But have you ever heard of a young boy being introduced to this concept? I mean, that means heteronormative sense, right? It's not logical that only young girls are subjected to the idea that their purity must be protected because if they were to have sex, they would have to be having sex *with* someone. So surely boys are also dealing with the shame and guilt of their budding sexualities, right?

Wrong, wrong, wrong. Of course it's wrong. As a living logical fallacy and complete contradiction, boys are generally not under the same pressure to remain virgins as young girls are. The good news for boys is that they don't have to accompany their mothers to a creepy purity ball. The bad news for boys is that they often deal with the negative stigma of being virgins. Boys are too often shamed for being virgins and girls are often shamed for *not* being virgins.

None of this makes sense, and all it does is make a difficult and awkward time even *more* difficult and awkward. What does make sense is to supply proper comprehensive sex education and responsibility to all sexes without shame.

The problem with putting so much pressure and emphasis on a girl's virginity is that it can lead to harmful—sometimes even physically harmful—and inhumane practices.

I attended an interim legislative session in the Kentucky state capitol one day to lobby for a gun reform bill. We were the last item on the agenda, so we waited as other groups and individuals lobbied state representatives and senators for the issues they care about—things like employee tobacco use laws, grandparent rights, etc.

Two women spoke on the subject of female genital mutilation (FGM) and it completely rocked my perspective of how the concept of purity harms girls and women as well as the scope of FGM. One woman represented the AHA Foundation, which is an organization in the pursuit of liberty from FGM, honor violence, and forced marriages. The founder of the organization is Ayaan Hirsi Ali. You may remember Ali from her 2007 autobiography, *Infidel*.

The other woman, Jennifer, was a survivor of FGM and she immediately addressed that she is not what you may have envisioned a survivor of FGM to be—white, Christian, barely in her forties, speaks with a bit of a Kentucky twang. I'll admit before hearing Jennifer's story, I thought FGM was something that happened far away and, even then, was pretty rare. I didn't realize it happened in my community.

Jennifer grew up in the Bible Belt and was raised in a conservative, evangelical church where her father also served as a minister. In this environment, a woman being sexual or having pleasure was considered sinful, like many, many other things were considered sinful. When she was five, she was told she and her sister were going on a special trip only to experience the unthinkable trauma of FGM.

As a result of the barbaric practice, Jennifer experienced many complications including chronic pain, persistent infections, painful sex, and an inability to birth her children vaginally. But Jennifer heroically spoke out about FGM and recounted a horrific story that still gives her flashbacks because so many girls are at risk of FGM. In the United States, there are roughly half a million girls at risk of FGM. Jennifer is lobbied the Kentucky state legislature because Kentucky was one of the twenty-three states in the United States that did not have laws protecting young girls and women from FGM. Jennifer was driven by the fear that she was not able to fully protect her own daughters from FGM without a law banning the practice.

Once again, a mom got it done. Jennifer and the team at the AHA Foundation were successful in their effort to convince the Kentucky legislature to ban FGM. The ban passed unanimously.

Currently, half a million (and that's a conservative estimate) girls are at risk of enduring a human rights violation right here in the United States. This is one example of how patriarchal attitudes oppressing women's sexuality savagely harms women.

Think about how the purity myth harms sexual assault survivors, whose bodies were violated and whose choices were taken from them. Now on top of the trauma, they struggle with the idea that they're no longer "pure" in the way they were taught they must be. How very cruel to teach young girls this bullshit concept while rape culture and purity culture chaotically coexist.

Women's bodies are not a currency to be traded for self-worth. So many things make up a woman's value and they're extremely individual—her compassion, her drive, her chutzpah, her spirit, her intelligence, her gifts, her humor, her bravery, her strength. A woman's value cannot be limited to her "sexual purity." And honestly? How *dare* anyone depreciate our value to something so small, minor, and insignificant.

We are not small. We know our worth and it is not determined by our sexual experience or inexperience. Sex is not a measure of morality. Let's stop teaching our daughters that their value is between their legs. So many other traits about your daughters make up their inherent worth, so go ahead and cross virginity off the list.

PART II

Self-Care

CHAPTER FIVE

What to Do When Mama Needs a Nap, but the Patriarchy Won't Smash Itself

I f there's one group who has the power to reject sexism and make a contribution to building a world that is kinder and more equal to women, it's mothers.

Look, it's not because "moms do it all!" and we do it all because "we're just so good at it!" That's a cop-out, and it's truly a bit insulting. We don't want groveling at our supposed superiority. We want things like equal pay and wouldn't mind more dresses with pockets.

Mothers can defeat sexism because they have power. Take a moment and consider the power you possess. You as a grown woman most likely have the power to vote, run for office, influence others, protest, and use your voice, among other things. But you as a mother have the great responsibility of raising the next generation.

Often in the daily, mundane cycle of mothering, you may not get a chance to think about the gravity of what you're *really* doing. You're not just packing lunches and shuffling kids to school, you're building the future of our world—every day. You're shaping your child's upbringing, which will shape their entire lives and then will contribute to our future. So much of how your children will change our world is being fostered right now—by *you*. It's an absolutely awe-inspiring power.

Just to demonstrate how great a mother's power is, let's take one example of your surface-level power as an example—voting. Since 1964, there have been more female voters than male. This isn't a fluke; it has happened consistently for decades. In recent elections, women have cast nearly ten million more votes than men. Almost ten million! Although it may not always show in terms of representation or topics discussed on the debate stage, women are the voting majority. We largely determine elections.

So, you may wonder if women have the power to determine elections, why has there *never* been a woman president? How do we now have a record number of women in Congress and they still represent less than a quarter of the House? Is it possible that women are participating in their own electoral oppression?

The quick and uncomfortable answer to that is, well...yes.

But let's backtrack a bit. Women in the United States indeed have a higher voter turnout than men. But it's also true that voter turnout is still just not great. The United States is among the worst in the developed world in terms of voter turnout; out of thirty-five countries, we rank thirty-first. Although it may appear that lazy Americans just couldn't be bothered to end their Netflix binges to vote for the first potential woman president, the truth is more complicated than that. In the United States, we don't make it easy to vote. (Half the time, voters don't even get those cute little Instagrammable

"I Voted" stickers!) In 2016, fourteen states enacted more restrictive voting laws all across the country such as limitations on voter registration, photo ID mandates, and narrower periods to vote on an already inconvenient day. (Tuesday, really?)

But, while some women were undoubtedly hindered by these laws, it is also probable that of the more than 43 percent of eligible voters who didn't vote in the 2016 election, many of them just chose not to. Even though women generally kick men's asses at turning up for elections, there's still a lot of women who didn't show.

Most women did indeed vote for Clinton in 2016, but to be fair, most Americans voted for Clinton in 2016 as Trump lost the popular vote. The largest voting bloc is a group of women, white women, and they voted for the Republican candidate.

The stark racial divide in 2016 showed the majority of white women, roughly 53 percent, voted for Trump. Among Latino women, only 25 percent voted for Trump. Even more amazing, among Black women, only 4 percent voted for Trump. It might as well have been just Diamond and Silk.

Women *have the power* to determine elections. But if we want our elected officials to be reflective of the people they represent and represent our interests, some things need to change:

+ We have to vote and stand against obstacles in the way of voting.

+ We have to change our attitudes and examine every candidate with a feminist lens, even if this means stepping outside party lines.

+ White women cannot depend on women of color to bail them out every election.

Voting is an attainable, accessible way we can exercise our power, and it should not be underestimated. As a collective force, we have the power to change our country and the world. And we can teach our children the importance of participating in our democracy and not voting for a candidate who is harmful to women.

This is not necessarily the same as voting Democrat or teaching our kids to vote Democrat. It's best to think critically and refuse to tolerate bigotry and misogyny in any candidate. So many women voted for Trump in 2016 because he had an "R" next to his name on the ballot. It turns out party lines are a hell of a drug. We cannot make this mistake again. Regardless of your political affiliation, if a sexual predator who is harmful to women and says terrible, racist, xenophobic things becomes the golden child of your party's ticket, it's time to denounce your party. Taking a stand against misogyny is worth your party losing an election.

The point is, we currently have this power to make a tremendous change. Voting is just one of many, many examples of ways we can exercise our power and teach our children to do the same. Things are not hopeless. We can singlehandedly put out this dumpster fire and turn this world into a place we're proud to inhabit.

The problem is...you're tired.

You're angry about the state of the world right now and you are passionate about advancing women's rights and defeating misogyny once and for all. But you're so damn *tired*. Sometimes, you catch yourself collapsing after carrying your mental and physical workload because it's just so heavy. Sometimes, you look away because you can't bear the constant news cycle of people hurt and dying all the time. Sometimes, you hide from your kids in the bathroom just because you need a couple of minutes of quiet.

I know. I get it. It's ok.

We need to find a way for you to fight for your beliefs and passions while protecting your safety and mental health. But don't worry, you can do anything, and I know you can do this.

Pick Three Things

The current news cycle in the United States too often reflects a country that is in so many ways broken. Every new development and news story is like an advancing disease that somehow coexists with comorbidities. Yet another mass shooting occurs, which reminds you of the overall epidemic of gun violence. Another state passes a law attempting to ultimately challenge Roe v. Wade, which reminds you of the nationwide attack on reproductive rights. Another soldier dies in Afghanistan, which reminds you—holy shit, we're still in Afghanistan?!

I understand the urge to unplug, and it can even be healthy sometimes! But ignoring the issues on a long-term basis only allows them to intensify. It's like if you catch your toddler in their room with an open Sharpie in their hand. You want to just close the door and walk away, but you know that's not going to help the situation. Your attention and passion for the issues you care about most are needed right now, and we can't afford for you to look away.

Let me guess—you look around your home and see problems that need to be fixed. You keep your kids' homework and permission slips from going astray. You seem to always come to a quick conflict resolution at work. When your kid is having a meltdown about wanting the blue sippy cup with stripes and not the one with polka dots, you find a way for him to make his peace with polka dots when no one else could. Although you have the power to fix a multitude of issues, you cannot singlehandedly solve the world's problems. Even Bill Gates has to focus on vaccines and mosquito nets.

Let's take the Gates as an example. I don't know about you, but I can hardly imagine taking a Target trip without scanning the Circle app for coupons. I cannot fathom having the wealth the Gates family has. With their insane amount of wealth and philanthropic resources, the Bill and Melinda Gates Foundation is the largest private foundation in the world.

Even better, super-rich people tend to have super-rich friends. Warren Buffet, who was at the time of his donation was literally the richest person in the world, is a trustee of the foundation and has made contributions worth billions of dollars. (Billions with a "b"!)

This organization has basically all the money and resources available that an organization could possibly have. But, to operate efficiently and make some type of positive difference, they have to narrow their focus to certain goals. In their case, that's enhancing healthcare, reducing extreme poverty, and expanding educational opportunities.

So, in their work, have they accomplished all their goals or just one goal? Have they completely eradicated extreme poverty? No. But have they made a positive difference in the areas they care most about? Absolutely.

Unless you have taken Warren Buffet's place as the richest person in the world, I'm going to assume you have less time and money than the Bill and Melinda Gates Foundation. They couldn't make a positive difference by playing Batman and just generally stating a goal that they wanted to make the world a better place. They needed to narrow their focus to accomplish some good, and so do you.

You cannot singlehandedly eradicate the world's issues. But can you, just like the Bill and Melinda Gates Foundation, narrow your focus to most efficiently advocate for the things you care about most and make a positive difference? Absolutely.

To do this, I have a challenge for you. Think about the issues you care most about. These are the issues that pull at your heartstrings and make you genuinely emotional, the ones that you always read articles about when they pop up in the news, and the ones that stir a wave of anger inside you that you don't know how to harness into some type of positive action. These are the issues you care about the most, and these are the ones that you should dedicate your time and energy toward. You can choose three of these prioritized issues, so choose carefully.

You may feel so passionate about these issues you've prioritized because they've personally affected you in some way or personally affect people you love. Access to healthcare may be a big one for you because you once experienced being uninsured and know what it's like to live without affordable access to care. Maybe climate change is important to you because you fear what kind of environment we're leaving for our children to inherit. These personal experiences and passions are so valuable in activism because they keep your fire burning and ignite a spark in others.

So I'm sorry to make things a bit more complicated. I'm going to add one more caveat. Make sure that the issues you choose don't only personally affect you. Choose issues that predominantly affect groups that you do not fall into.

This caveat is not just because I think you're up for the challenge. The reason is that if people only act in their self-interest, marginalized groups will undoubtedly be left behind. We see this all the time in countless areas. Think about a woman going missing, who do you think of—Laci Peterson, maybe Natalee Holloway? Whoever she is, she's probably pretty and white because those are the missing persons' cases that get the most attention on the six o'clock news and the ire of Nancy Grace.

There's even a term for this media and public phenomenon: "Missing White Women Syndrome." Do you remember the case of the Philadelphia woman, LaToyia Figueroa, who was five-months pregnant when she was reported missing? Probably not, because the case didn't get national media attention like the cases involving white women. This is what happens to issues when people only care about themselves and people like them. To exercise true compassion, we must care for others when we have nothing to gain ourselves. We must keep ourselves accountable and ensure we're not concerned with only our self-interest.

I think part of exercising anti-racism is being candid and not dancing around difficult subjects. So, please allow me to be frank. I'm talking about giving your attention to issues that affect everyone, to avoid focusing on white people issues, and to stop ignoring issues until they begin affecting white people. If you are concerned about gun violence, for example, please don't only focus on preventing school shootings when Black children are ten times more likely to be killed by gun violence than white children.

When choosing your issues, you can make them general or narrow the focus according to the time and mental energy you have to devote to the issue. For example, you can choose an umbrella term such as immigration and that can be one of your three issues, knowing that immigration is frequently in the news and there are many, many facets to the issue that will occupy your time. You know best what you can and are willing to handle.

Your top three issues can be in flux. I never imagined dismantling a federal agency would be one of my top issues. But once I began hearing of children being detained at the United States and Mexico border in glorified cages and indefinitely separated from their families, that unimaginable cruelty influenced my support of the abolition of Immigration and Customs Enforcement (ICE), which is now one of my top three under the umbrella of defeating white supremacy.

Your top three issues are the ones you're devoting yourself to—your volunteer hours, your monetary contributions, your emotional state, your social media shares, your opinions, and so on. This doesn't mean you can't care or have opinions about other issues, of course you will! But the way you express yourself with those other issues will manifest in different ways that are less demanding of your time, such as voting.

Prioritizing your passions will help you be a more efficient activist while fitting activism into your workload without overwhelming you.

Not All Self-Care Happens Is a Bubble Bath

A few years ago, I was having a rough time. I was physically and mentally unwell. I was a stay-at-home mom, and yet I was more stressed than I'd ever been with any other job. I was overwhelmed by the gravity of being a mother and everything raising little humans entailed. I was always needed, and yet somehow so lonely. I was tired in a way that no amount of sleep could ever help.

I was not taking care of myself. But the thing is, I was taking the time to do everything I thought self-care involved. I took the occasional solo trip to Target and sometimes even bought a latte while I was out. I went on vacation with my family to beautiful places. My husband and I went on regular date nights. I even did what I thought was the epitome of self-care, I took bubble baths. Not just bubble baths, but baths with the jets on, candles lit, a colorful bath bomb that a Lush employee told me was kissed by a unicorn or something, the whole thing.

It wasn't enough.

On the flight home from a family vacation or trip away, I would already be thinking about where to go next. I do love to travel, but I realized that what I thought was exercising good self-care habits was just distraction from what was really bothering me. I didn't need to escape, whether it was to a tropical location or just my bathroom. I needed to change my life to one I didn't need to escape from.

This was the most beneficial self-care I had ever done. I did a lot of introspective hard work and asked myself tough questions I previously avoided like, "What do you want to do with your life?" (still working on that one) and "What is keeping you up at night?" There are things we're capable of controlling and things we're not. But when I took inventory of the things that made me unhappy, I realized it was possible to change. Sure, it was going to involve a lot of hard work, but it wasn't impossible. I had control.

So I examined the issues in my life that made me want to escape—the tensions, the unfinished tasks, the abandoned dreams—and planned to resolve them. The solutions varied from getting proper medical care and medication to spending time with friends who made me feel good. I even explored my unfulfilled dreams like the one I've had my entire life, to write a book. I identified the steps to make that dream a reality. Then I slowly achieved each goal on the path to publication. And I'll be damned if I'm not here writing this book!

I still love my bubble baths with fizzy, fragrant bath bombs. I still have an unrelenting travel bug. All these little breaks are welcomed little bits of my self-care routine. But for me, the real self-care was the result of investing in myself, knowing my self-worth, doing extremely hard things, and believing in my ability to do hard things.

Self-care is vital. It's so much more than little slices of cucumber on your eyes. It's self-preservation. You don't just want time to yourself or to make yourself a priority, you need to. I've been on enough trips to hear the flight attendant instruct everyone to put on their own oxygen masks before helping others. You need to take care of yourself first so you're in the best place to take care of your family.

But when you're making the time for self-care, consider what is it you need. Do you need to grab margaritas with the girls, or do you need therapy with a licensed professional? Do you need a mani-pedi, or do you need to talk to your spouse about your feelings? Do you need just a few minutes of solitude hiding in the pantry, or do you need to reassess your career goals?

Have the courage to ask yourself the difficult questions you've possibly avoided. Your thoughts, your dreams, your goals, your desires—they all matter. YOU matter. Taking the time to care for yourself and reflect on what you need is worth your time.

Writer and feminist legend Audre Lorde understood that self-care was much deeper than the hashtag on Instagram portrays. Lorde called the caring of one's self an "act of political warfare." Honestly, how badass is that? Self-care is a radical act in which you declare that you matter in a world that too often insists you don't.

When you're engaged in social justice and the pursuit of equality, you're also engrossed in what often feels like an endless cycle of terrible, terrible news. At the very least, it can be disheartening to see what a daunting task we have ahead of us. At worst, it can reactivate trauma. To keep pressing on, you must exercise self-preservation. You must develop coping mechanisms that allow you to be an effective activist and maintain your sanity.

The balance between taking care of yourself and taking care of others is a delicate, but attainable one. You just need to make the conscious effort and decision to put yourself as a top priority. Give yourself the grace of knowing that you matter, be kind to yourself, and be mindful of your needs.

What It Really Means to Be Triggered

In their constant battle to "own the libs," the far-right tends to dismiss the very real feelings of those rightfully offended. They whine that they're "not allowed to speak their mind" anymore and people are just "so easily offended" now instead of considering that it's reasonable to be hurt when someone disparages your race, sex, religion, and who you are as a person.

What a load of horse shit. No—elephant shit. A huge, huge amount of elephant shit. The First Amendment is alive and well in the United States. I mean, other than the president of the United States' constant assault on the free press and blocking Twitter users who criticize him, our freedom of speech is pretty solid and anyone in the United States is free to say whatever silly, offensive thing they wish to say.

But freedom of speech does not equate to freedom of consequences and sometimes consequences do occur as a result of saying terrible things. Like that time white nationalist golden boy, Richard Spencer got punched in the face. Spencer has the constitutionally protected right to march around and say horrible, racist, anti-Semitic things. But that does carry the risk of being punched in the face.

Conservative pundits have hijacked the word "triggered" to essentially mean "offended." This word is used often in memes portraying bright-haired feminists looking aggravated. It's used in completely fabricated anti-feminist tales like, *"Oh, no. Don't want to trigger the feminists by holding a door open for a woman."* Feminists are way too concerned about the pursuit of equal pay and pockets to care whether or not a door is left open for them.

But triggers are real. The phrase "trigger" is a clinical term that mental health professionals use to describe a stimulus that causes someone to have an emotional or physical response related to their previous trauma. A trigger often sets off a memory and takes the person back to a traumatic event in the form of flashbacks. A trigger can be many different things—a smell, sound, or sight—anything that stimulates the person's senses in a way that causes them to relive their trauma.

My husband is an Army veteran and a psychotherapist who treats other vets like himself. I proofread his papers while he was in grad school, so although this didn't earn me any type of honorary degree, I have some familiarity with triggers and how they relate to post-traumatic stress disorder.

Service members in the military who have served in combat often have experienced some level of trauma. Of the veterans who served in the conflicts in Iraq and Afghanistan, between 11 and 20 percent are diagnosed with PTSD in any given year. So PTSD is not uncommon and tends to manifest in many different ways. Identifying triggers to trauma responses is a big part of cognitive-behavioral therapy to treat PTSD. If a vet has PTSD, through their work in therapy they may have identified that driving on a certain stretch of highway is a trigger for them because it brings them back to surviving an IED blast during a convoy in Iraq.

Although military experience is often where someone's mind wanders when thinking of PTSD, it's not the only or even most common cause. Of those in the United States who have PTSD, about 50 percent of the related trauma is related to physical or sexual violence. Although men and boys are survivors of sexual violence and it often goes unreported, most survivors of sexual violence in the United States are women. Nearly 44 percent of women in the United States experience some form of sexual violence in their lifetime.

So, when we talk about triggers, it's largely an issue that affects women. Even if a woman is not in therapy at the time or if she hasn't had an opportunity to be diagnosed with PTSD, she could have self-identified her triggers. Hearing details of a sexual assault may understandably be a trigger for a woman who survived sexual assault and has lingering post-traumatic stress as a result.

If someone is "triggered," they're not merely offended by a political position as some conservative commentators suggest. They're reliving the absolute worst part of their entire lives— often in a literal sense through flashbacks—and they truly feel as if a traumatic event is happening again. This is an enormous weight to carry, and to minimize this struggle isn't just foolish, it's incredibly cruel.

You may have survived some type of trauma and have personally identified triggers of your own. Sexual predators finally getting their days in court provides us with some semblance of justice and hope, but the ongoing news cycle recounting their horrific crimes can be an absolute nightmare for those with triggers involving sexual assault. Imagine how many hearts begin racing every time Harvey Weinstein is in the news.

If triggers affect you, please don't allow any callous fools to dismiss your very real struggles. There are options such as therapy available so you can help manage your triggers and symptoms. Unfortunately, I understand that because we don't live in a land that prioritizes mental health access and affordable health care, it's possible that therapy is not attainable to you, and I do understand that simply advising you to "go get therapy" isn't helpful. So let's keep it simple. You know yourself and how things make you feel. If you choose to avoid certain content because it provokes a negative emotional response, that is ok.

If you already carry that weight, there is no need to add to the load. Just because you want to stop sexual abuse, you do not have to constantly subject yourself to hearing about the horrors of sexual abuse. You do not need to witness horror after horror just because you want to stop horrific things from happening. Know your limits.

Father Jeremy Richman survived the most unimaginable nightmare of every parent when he lost his six-year-old daughter, Avielle, in the school shooting at Sandy Hook Elementary. Along with his wife, Jeremy began the work of preventing further violence with their nonprofit The Avielle Foundation. Seven years after the shooting, Jeremy died by suicide as his wife explained that he succumbed to the grief he could not escape.

I tell you about Jeremy because activism can be rewarding, powerful, extremely difficult, and mentally taxing work. When we talk about trauma, there's no understating the harm it can cause: it can be life or death. You must manage your mental health along with your passions. When the passions behind your advocacy are associated with previous trauma you've survived, please be aware of your mental well-being at all times. Prioritize managing your mental health in whatever way you see fit.

If things ever get too heavy and you need support, reach out to talk to someone you love and trust or find a mental health professional. You have so much to offer this wild world, and we need you here.

Saying No

Throughout my life, I've struggled with my natural inclination to be a "people pleaser." I never thought this would be a behavior I would want to stop. I thought it was a positive attribute. I've come from a long line of "people pleasers" and "hard workers," so I inherited a strong desire to make others happy and will tirelessly work to do so with great enthusiasm.

A natural desire to be kind and help others *is* positive. The world seems to be in a constant kindness deficit. We need more enthusiastic people willing to put in the work to make a change. So if you label yourself a natural people pleaser, your compassion and dedication will be assets to you and the movements you support.

But in a world that values the constant grind of hustle culture and being perpetually busy, tacking people-pleasing traits on top will only result in your total mental and physical exhaustion as a result of accumulating pressure. It may seem like a harmless act of altruism, but being a people pleaser is a toxic habit that pleases no one, least of all yourself.

If you have some people-pleasing habits, think about what you're really seeking. It's probably not simply a desire to make everyone happy. For one, that's a futile mission that is a complete waste of your time. You can't make everyone happy—you're not cheesecake. Is it something else you're looking for—validation, the feeling of being needed, approval?

Are alarm bells in your head going off? Ok. I assure you the validation you may seek from pleasing others will not be near as fulfilling as granting that validation and grace to yourself. If you're seeking to please someone, you need to put yourself much higher on the list than your neighbor Carol who wants you to volunteer for the HOA board.

Part of breaking these toxic habits is prioritizing. Now, you've already done this. You have identified your top three issues that are the most important to you. You also understand the importance of self-care and love. So, if you're asked to do something that is not among your top priorities, not the best use of your time and mental energy, or just simply something you do not want to do, how do you respond? Just say no.

When someone asks something of you, it's not mandatory. You always have choices, and saying no is a valid option. Respect yourself and your time while insisting that others grant you the same courtesy. Every time you are given an opportunity, carefully consider it and how it would potentially influence your current workload. If your heart immediately starts pumping with anxiety thinking about how you would handle it, understand that you can decline.

No in itself is a complete sentence. So if you decline something, you don't need to elaborate. You don't need to explain that you're already so overwhelmed with so many other tasks that you now only sleep thirty-five minutes a night. You don't have to wait until you're completely drained to begin saying no. It's valid to just say no because you're already too busy. It's valid to say no because saying yes would cut into your time watching the *Real Housewives of Orange County* and you want to see if Vicki and Tamra are friends right now.

When considering your current and future workload, think about what tasks you can delegate to others. You can apply this to all facets of your life. If you're volunteering your time to a cause you care about deeply, but you're unsure if you're the right person to oversee certain tasks, consider delegating those tasks to someone else who would be a better fit. If you find yourself being the only one in your household cleaning, consider that, "Oh! Wait! Other people live in this house too!" and feel free to hand them a dust mop. I do not doubt that you are excellent at everything you do, but that doesn't mean you have to do everything. Even small children can learn to clean up after themselves. You don't have to do it all.

I understand this may feel a bit contradictory, considering much of the current movement to defeat bigotry and misogyny is built by busy moms who frankly don't have time for it. Even co-chair of the inaugural march and mom Linda Sarsour said in an interview that she really didn't have time, but felt she had little choice as this was so important. The day after Trump's inauguration at the first Women's March, I noticed a lot of women whose anger was focused on the current state of affairs. But I also saw a lot of women who were angry that they even needed to be there. Women were marching who would rather spend their Saturday afternoon enjoying a rigorous Netflix binge. There were women my grandmother's age holding signs that said, "I can't believe I still have to protest this shit."

We still have to protest this shit. I hope by the time I reach my grandmother's age, I spend my Saturdays crafting vulgar needlepoint and napping because misogyny and bigotry have long since been defeated and we finally live in a utopian society with equality and flying cars! But we're not there yet.

So, to be clear, I'm not asking you to say no to everything. But I am enforcing the idea that saying no is always, always an option for whatever reason. Even if you're presented with an opportunity to help with a cause that is aligned with your top priorities, if it's not something you can enthusiastically say yes to right now, it's ok to say no.

I would especially encourage you to say no to the things that suck up your time, leaving you feeling drained and defeated with little return. Say no to futile conversations with people who challenge your political positions. You don't owe anyone a debate. If you enjoy political discourse and the conversation is respectful, go ahead. If you just take the occasional simple pleasure in laying an intellectual smackdown on someone who challenged your way of thinking, ok, sure, have fun.

But, if your weird uncle wants to chat about current events using rhetoric and conspiracy theories he just picked up from Alex Jones while you're trying to enjoy Thanksgiving dinner, feel free to pass. Also, I just recently discovered when people comment online who disagree with your opinion, you can just ignore it. I started practicing the art of ignoring replies (especially on articles, comments, and Twitter threads), and WOW, is it liberating. Someone disagreeing with you does not make your opinion any less valid. You are free to express whatever opinion you'd like, and there is not a punishment that you must reply thoughtfully to every mansplaining goof demanding a debate. Just turn off notifications and walk away.

You know yourself and what you can comfortably handle. Set firm boundaries about saying no to what isn't productive or good for you. Stick to your priorities and stay focused to remain the most effective champion you can be for the causes you care about most. Love and take care of yourself as Audre Lorde intended—as an act of political warfare. We need you in these battles rested, able, and ready to fight.

CHAPTER SIX

Motherhood–American Style!

I sat upright in my hospital bed with my second born, a daughter, rested on my bare chest where my hospital gown was left slightly open. I couldn't stop smiling as I held her little fists in my hands and gazed as her sweet little face in absolute wonder.

For me, pregnancy and childbirth weren't things I enjoyed, they were things I endured because I wanted so desperately to be a mother and have babies to love. I was a high-risk patient and my pregnancies were full of medical complications and worry. With my first, I had gone into pre-term labor about halfway through my pregnancy. Then I remained on bedrest while I fought gestational diabetes and a baby that was just really anxious to be earth-side before his time. But after a grueling labor and delivery, my beautiful son was born at thirty-six weeks. I was able to take him directly home from the hospital without even a pit-stop at the NICU, which I know is such a blessing.

My perinatologist let me know that I was quite bad at being pregnant and birthing babies. I'm sure he worded it a bit more gently, but that was the gist. Combined with some other health concerns, it was recommended to me, if I wanted more

children, to try for one more in the next few years. But after
that one, the baby factory needed to be closed.

I was elated to be pregnant with my second. I knew I'd likely
have a trying journey ahead, but I just kept thinking about the
day I could finally hold that precious baby in my arms. A nurse
came to my home to administer weekly progesterone shots to
prevent my stubborn one from trying to be born before the
right time. But I went into pre-term labor just like the first
pregnancy. Otherwise, my previous complications didn't arise,
and instead, I had exciting new complications! My pregnancies
were so different, a nurse practitioner asked if it was the same
father. I joked that I thought so, which was met with no laughs.

I felt so betrayed by my own body. I felt as if everything about
becoming a mother and having my babies was such a challenge
from the dozens of negative home pregnancy tests to my own
womb's inability to remain a refuge. I could handle the pain;
I could handle any pain if it just meant I'd be holding my
baby soon.

So, finally, when I held that baby on my chest, it was magical,
and I was so intensely grateful that we made it. She was here!
She was perfect. She was mine. I allowed myself to wail and
release tears of joy and relief right along with her cries.

Right after birth, I had a postpartum hemorrhage. This is not
an entirely uncommon complication and has many different
causes, as well as some unidentified causes, so it can affect
many women without warning. With treatment, it typically
doesn't cause any further complications, but left untreated, it
can cause shock or death. About 1 to 5 percent of women have
a postpartum hemorrhage, and it's more likely with cesarean
births. It can also happen with vaginal births like mine. Of
all the things that happened throughout my pregnancy and

childbirth, the hemorrhage was among the least eventful and memorable. I barely even remember hearing that I had hemorrhaged because I was so focused on my new baby. The baby was out, healthy, plump, and perfect. That was all I cared about.

My husband and I spent the first hour after birth taking our time and introducing our new daughter to Earth. She seemed to like it here. I was amazed at how she latched on and nursed mere *minutes* after being born. It was just incredible to me.

Then after that hour, we invited our ecstatic family members who had been anxiously sitting in the waiting room into the hospital room to meet our new daughter. I was sitting in the bed holding her tight and smiling proudly as our family members oohed and ahhed. From the moment she was born, I held and nuzzled her so tightly because this was the moment I had dreamt about my entire pregnancy. But suddenly no matter how hard I tried to hang on, I felt my grip loosen as she began falling from my arms to the bed.

Then everything went black.

The first thing I saw when I regained consciousness was the doctor who delivered my baby. I felt so cold and couldn't stop shaking, and I didn't quite have the strength to speak or move. I was able to open my eyes and I could hear. I looked to see my husband, who sat in the corner with a new baby swaddled in his arms looking terrified. Then I looked at the doctor, who held an iPhone in her hand and said, "I'm not sure what's happening. I'm going to Google it."

Y'all. She was going to *Google it*. Here I am, lying in a hospital bed, thinking, *Well. This is how it ends, folks. Died after childbirth due to the hospital's shitty Wi-Fi signal.*

Fortunately, the Wi-Fi signal must have been strong that day, and the doctor revived me from shock relatively quickly. I had a blood transfusion (thanks, blood donors!) as I held my newborn daughter, and I lived to tell the tale about my brush with maternal mortality.

Of all of the worries I had during my pregnancies, I'll admit dying as a result of childbirth wasn't one of them. I thought dying this way was mainly a literary device reserved for classics like *Oliver Twist*, not something that rarely happened in modern society.

But what I discovered after the births of my children is that maternal mortality is a huge, horrific problem in the United States. The US spends more on health care than any other country, but the United States also has the highest rate of maternal mortality in the developed world. Not only is the state of maternal mortality dire in the US, but it also keeps getting worse—much worse. The maternal mortality rate has more than doubled from 10.3 per 100,000 live births in 1991 to 23.8 in 2014.

Although the rate of maternal mortality in the United States overall is catastrophic. It varies from state to state. In Indiana, where I gave birth, mothers die in childbirth at eleven times the rate as mothers in California. Mothers in Indiana, Iraq, and the Gaza Strip have roughly the same maternal mortality rate. In 2011, the year before I had my first child, the state of Indiana experienced a devastating increase in mothers dying as a result of childbirth. The year 2011 happened to be the same year the elected government of the state began their assault on women's health through the defamation of institutions providing vital women's health services like Planned Parenthood and began a famine of public health funding.

The crux of the attack on women's healthcare, which the
state of Indiana has still not recovered from, was a bill
blocking federal funds from going to Planned Parenthood and
specifically prohibiting Planned Parenthood from providing
any services via Medicaid. This was a tale as old as time, a
bunch of old white dudes at the statehouse governing women's
bodies because they claim to want to stop abortion. The law
was even deemed unconstitutional, but half of the Planned
Parenthood clinics in the state closed as a result. (None of
which performed abortions, by the way.) Oh, and do you know
who authored that bill? None other than (hopefully former by
the time you read this) Vice President Mike Pence.

What is so heartbreakingly maddening about the issue of
maternal mortality is that the causes are generally consistent.
So, it's no mystery. One of the most common causes is
hemorrhage, as I experienced. Other causes include sepsis,
embolism, and cardiovascular events. Only about 6 percent
of maternal mortality cases have no known cause. Due to this
predictability, 60 percent of maternal mortality deaths are
completely preventable.

Other than the fact that I lived in a country with a high
maternal mortality rate and a state that is among the worst
in the country, I didn't personally have many risk factors. I
wasn't reliant on healthcare through programs like Medicaid
or Planned Parenthood. I didn't live in a very rural area, where
mothers often have a lack of accessible care and a higher risk of
maternal mortality. Also, I'm white.

Like so many other issues, white women undoubtedly
experience them, but not nearly to the level of women of color.
Black mothers have the greatest risk of maternal mortality.
Black mothers succumb to maternal mortality at a rate of 3.3

times greater than white mothers. Native American or Alaskan Native women have a maternal mortality rate of 2.5 times greater than white mothers. So, yes, I was one of the lucky ones, but as a white woman, those odds were in my favor.

Maternal mortality is one glaring issue that shines a light on the hypocrisy in the United States: we think mothers are so honored and revered, but based on how we treat mothers in this country, this cannot be true. We cannot say the United States honors and loves mothers while we allow so many of them to die in the process.

Motherhood is often viewed as a natural rite of passage for every woman. Women are constantly asked, "Do you want kids?" "When do you want to have kids?" "Do you want more kids?" and "Isn't that too many kids?" Then once they reach the ripe age of thirty, women receive ominous warnings about their "biological clocks" ticking, which I imagine must be something like the ticking crocodile in Peter Pan which only meddlesome people can hear.

On a superficial level, it appears we love mothers in the United States. Conservatives often tout "traditional" family values with the mother as a nurturing, integral force. Dozens of people protest outside abortion clinics regularly just for the chance to plead with a woman not to have the procedure. They'll spend hours waiting for that exchange lasting mere seconds because they feel so strongly about preserving motherhood and that woman carrying her pregnancy to term.

So, you would think that if motherhood is so revered, that adoration would extend far beyond the pregnancy. But, although we put so much emphasis on the value of motherhood and encourage essentially every woman of childbearing age to become a mother, we also make being a mother exceedingly difficult.

Women's healthcare is constantly being debated on the floors of state capitols and in Congress. While the debate is always centered on conservatives' desperate desire to save babies and protect mothers, the resulting legislation and stigma it promotes harm women. Pence's bill, which anti-abortion activists celebrated, was followed by a sharp increase in maternal mortality. Now, I understand that correlation does not imply causation, but just imagine me gesturing vaguely to suffering mothers all over this country.

The United States is the only developed country in the world that does not grant paid maternity leave, placing a serious undue financial burden on families. The cost of childcare is astronomical, which again financially burdens families and often influences a mother's decision to stay at home. The majority of millennial mothers feel discouraged when it comes to managing their careers and families.

The majority of young mothers also handle the majority of household chores and responsibilities. Who makes your child's doctor's appointments? Well, if you're like the 93 percent of millennial moms, you do. That's just one task. Think about what the average mom's physical and mental workload involves.

And ugh, do we even need to discuss the state of healthcare in this country? I mean, the fact that mothers are dying at the highest rate in the developed world gives us a clue that our healthcare is pretty fucked. But we're also lacking proper postpartum care and not receiving thorough screening for postpartum mood disorders. We treat proper healthcare as an unachievable pipedream, but other countries prioritize maternal health and manage to achieve what we don't even attempt.

In the United States, when millennial mothers were asked if they feel supported and understood by society, 85 percent said no. And honestly, why would they? Where's the support and understanding—somewhere in between the lack of accessible healthcare and financial stress?

The state of motherhood in the United States does not have to be so dire. We know the factors that make motherhood so unnecessarily bleak and we can work to repair them. Motherhood is hard, but it doesn't have to be this hard.

Stop Politically Policing Our Bodies

As a millennial, I don't remember a time when reproductive healthcare was not a hot political topic. As soon as I was introduced to politics, I heard candidates discuss their stance on abortion. Even for my high school age peers, it was one of the first opinion positions they formed, which then evolved into their party affiliations. I can't even count how many times abortion has come up in conversation—seldom as a personal experience, but always as a political stance. But few other political positions are given the same amount of attention and fervor.

Now abortion is an incredibly divisive and partisan issue, which is often presented as an issue of morality rather than a political one. The few abortion clinics operating do so with a regular crowd of protestors and so-called "sidewalk counselors" who plead with patients not to enter the clinic. It's an expected topic for political debate, and misinformation whirls around as polarizing political candidates repeat wild claims such as abortions regularly occurring days before the due dates. (That doesn't happen.)

So, I was shocked to learn that there was once a time when abortion was not treated with this level of political consideration and significance. After Roe v. Wade was established as law of the land, Republicans largely honored that law by valuing individual freedom over mandating a woman's choice. Abortion was generally viewed as a private matter that was just part of life, an inevitable occurrence. In 1972, the year before Roe, 68 percent of Republicans believed the decision of whether or not to have an abortion should be left to a woman and her doctor. In 2019, only 36 percent of Republicans share that belief.

Before Ronald Reagan's presidential campaign, if he had such strong, moral opposition to abortion, he sure had a funny way of showing it. As governor of California, the Gipper signed into law an abortion bill before Roe v. Wade. That law resulted in more than one million abortions. MORE. THAN. ONE. MILLION. ABORTIONS.

Now surely, the patriarch of the Republican party wouldn't simply pretend to have a moral authority regarding abortion in an attempt to sway evangelical voters, right? Well, regardless of his candid thoughts on the subject, the tactic of appealing to the religious right with fundamental social issues certainly worked. Reagan's presidential campaign was a revolutionary moment in courting evangelical voters with anti-women rhetoric. That tactic is still used today as single-issue voters fight for moral high ground by fighting to deny women their reproductive rights.

Propaganda and deceit are used to vilify institutions women depend on, such as Planned Parenthood, as anti-choice lawmakers legislate women's bodies. Just as Pence's bill in Indiana was followed by a sharp increase in the rate of maternal mortality, these anti-choice laws are nonsensical and only result in harming women. Many Planned Parenthood clinics don't even provide abortion services, but they do provide life-saving mammograms, pap smears, STD screening, maternity care, and more. So, when the clinics close due to a lack of funding caused by anti-choice legislation, women who need access to care most are left without it.

Abortion is but a small piece of reproductive healthcare. By continuing to pass legislation restricting access to abortion, our government also denies women access to comprehensive care. It's like burning your house down because you disliked the carpet in the living room.

I know abortion providers and those seeking abortions are hit hardest by these restrictive measures. Doctors who took an oath to provide care to their patients are in danger simply by reporting to work. Tragedies like the assassination of Dr. George Tiller are a sober reminder of their vulnerability. Employees of the clinics and clinic escorts who volunteer their time to guide women into the clinic through the crowd of protestors face similar risk and hostility. The patients seeking abortions must find a clinic that is abortion-providing and not an anti-abortion ruse, then pay a decent sum of money because their health care may not cover it, then possibly travel because there aren't many clinics available anymore, then finally endure the mob of anti-abortion protestors shouting at them not to go into the clinic. So, anti-abortion legislation has not eliminated abortion, but there's no doubt it has made obtaining a safe, legal abortion more difficult.

Anti-choice bills are often not based in fact. In 2019, Ohio Governor Mike DeWine proudly signed one of the most severe abortion bans ever proposed. The bill orders physicians to "re-implant ectopic pregnancies" into a woman's uterus. If they do not, the physicians will face criminal charges up to and including *murder*. To be clear, an ectopic pregnancy is a nonviable pregnancy as the fertilized egg is located somewhere outside the womb. The biggest problem with the bill is that this directive is fucking impossible. Obstetricians and gynecologists took time away from treating women to tell a bunch of hard-headed lawmakers, that's not how it works. In response to the much-deserved backlash, the Republican representative who wrote the bill admitted he did so with anti-abortion lobbyists, didn't do any research into whether or not it was possible, and generally didn't know what the hell he was talking about.

Legislators are so committed to policing women's bodies, they'll just make shit up. Blessed be the fruit.

In addition to restricting abortion access, the lack of reproductive care also leaves women at a greater risk of maternal mortality, cervical cancer, breast cancer, STDs, and unplanned pregnancies. Planned Parenthood is not just an abortion provider, it's a place where women can receive affordable, factual, evidence-based healthcare without judgment. But anti-choice legislators don't want women to have that.

Women are still getting legal and safe abortions. They're just jumping through a lot of hoops on the way. It's not an effective method of eliminating abortions. Logic may guide you to think that if you want to reduce the number of abortions, reduce the number of unplanned pregnancies by making birth control accessible. But instead, under the current political pressure, all reproductive healthcare suffers.

Women suffer.

Legislating women's bodies harms women. We have to dissolve this idea that mandating what a woman does with her body is a matter of morality. It isn't. It wasn't until a man thought it would be a good way to manipulate evangelical voters, and women have been paying the price ever since.

Beyond the harmful aftermath of passing restrictive legislation, the root is deeply misogynistic. Women are not to be trusted with making decisions regarding their bodies. The purpose of childbearing is given more prominence than a woman's purpose of being.

Before politicians like Reagan turned women's healthcare into a partisan and political issue, it was viewed as a small, private matter. We need to return to this way of thinking. A woman's decision whether or not to obtain an abortion is much more nuanced than could ever be debated on a congressional floor.

The decision should not be debated at all. It should be a decision a woman can be trusted to make about her own body and her own life.

There's a misconception that women who have abortions do so to avoid motherhood. But the majority—59 percent—of women who obtain abortions are already mothers. Additionally, nearly one-quarter of all women in the United States will have an abortion before they turn forty-five.

When we talk about abortion, we're talking about something many mothers have chosen. Maybe you haven't personally had an abortion, but I'm sure you know someone who has. Whether or not they speak openly about their experience, they hear you. They hear everyone. They know the debate that rages about their decisions.

As a journalist, I once covered the ongoing conflict between anti-abortion protestors and pro-choice clinic escorts outside a state's sole abortion clinic for my city's alt-weekly. Abortions were only provided twice a week, and the clinic only saw maybe a handful of patients per day. The moment when a patient arrived, there was a sudden, discernible tension among the dozens of anti-abortion protestors and pro-choice clinic escorts.

A clinic escort recalled a time when a young woman and someone who appeared to be her male partner arrived in front of the clinic. The anti-abortion protestors swarmed the car and prepared to make their brief, but ardent case for not entering the clinic while holding signs showing graphic images of allegedly aborted fetuses.

At the same time, the clinic escorts swarmed the car donning their bright, reflective vests. An escort explained if the patient would like to be guided through the boisterous herd and to the clinic doors, they would be happy to do that.

"But why?" the patient asked, looking appalled and confused.

"Well, this is an issue that many people have strong feelings about," the escort attempted to quickly explain.

"But what do they have against Lasik?!" the patient asked, looking even more confused.

The abortion clinic happened to neighbor an optometrist.

It was an absurd scenario, but dictating whether or not a woman undergoes a medical procedure is also absurd. Beyond the woman herself and her doctor, no one has the knowledge or right to make that decision for her.

Roe remains law of the land at the federal level. But states constantly pass laws to undermine and ultimately defeat Roe. These are laws that harm women. Be vigilant of reproductive action happening in your state, and contact your representatives urging them not to vote for these bills that are so detrimental to women.

When reproductive rights are discussed with your friends, family, and community members, talk about these issues. Don't allow the rhetoric to be unchecked and infiltrate other women's positions on the issue. Share factual information about how attempts to restrict abortion access have harmed women far beyond their right to choose.

Keep your legislators accountable for how they treat women. This isn't an issue solely reserved for Republicans; Democrats sometimes concede to anti-abortion lobbyists as well. Remember a legislator's positions and actions in office regarding this issue when you vote.

As mothers and as women, we must demand that women are trusted to make decisions regarding their bodies. We have to stand for reproductive rights—all reproductive rights—and this includes unapologetically supporting a woman's right to choose.

Ask for More

We deserve more than we're getting right now. The weight of a household should not fall solely upon one mother. Hiding in the pantry stress eating Twizzlers is not self-care. A mother's career should not be more disturbed by parenthood than a father's. We need more support in our homes, our relationships, our healthcare, our workplaces, and our legislation. We know what we want and what we need to evolve American motherhood; now in all of our circles, we need to firmly ask for it.

When you look at your growing to-do list that involves all of your typical household and parenting tasks and start feeling overwhelmed by all that you have to do, ask yourself if it really needs to be you who does it.

Talk to your partner about your workload. Be honest about how overwhelmed you're feeling and how you can help each other out. Unless you both are around each other every hour of every day, you probably don't understand your partner's complete workload. Be specific and leave the conversation with specific action items to help each other. It may be that one of you doesn't mind doing laundry at all, but delegating that task brings huge relief to the other person.

If you need a break, specifically ask for a break. You don't need to justify it. You don't need to list the myriad reasons you're exhausted and deserving of a break. Just explicitly state, "Hey, I need a break, so I'm going to TJ Maxx and I'm going to smell candles for an hour. Please do not contact me unless you're following an ambulance." Direct, honest, to the point.

Likewise, give that same respect to your partner. Whether you stay at home with the kids or work outside the home, parenthood is hard, and it takes a toll on everyone. So, just check in with your partner occasionally and see how they're doing, how they're managing their workload, and if they need to delegate some tasks to help keep themselves afloat.

Illogically, kids love making messes *and* enjoy accomplishing small tasks. Have you ever entered a daycare or classroom and noticed that it somehow doesn't look like twenty pint-sized toddler tornados have just wreaked havoc all day in there? Part of the reason has to be that teachers are miracle workers and possess power most of us do not. But a big part of the reason is that teachers give the children, even very small children, the responsibility of tidying up after themselves and other tasks. Then they praise them for completing the tasks and the kids feel accomplished and proud of themselves. You can utilize that same tactic in your home and delegate small tasks to your kids that you know they can manage such as grabbing their own snacks and picking up their own little messes.

When it comes to asking for more in your place of work, the first thing you need to do is know your rights. For example, if you're breastfeeding, look up the laws in your state that grant you the opportunity to pump. (Usually, your employer needs to provide time and a clean, private room that is not a restroom.) Also, be familiar with the laws in your state regarding maternity leave, discrimination, the Family and Medical Leave Act, and any other laws regarding pregnancy or motherhood. Your legal rights are the bare minimum that an employer should give you as a mother, and they are not optional. If your rights at work are being threatened, your knowledge of your rights will help you defend yourself. Hopefully, you have a family-friendly employer and none of these issues arise, but if they do, you'll be prepared.

Once you know your rights, you'll be armed with the information you need to ensure you have the accommodations you're entitled to. No pun intended, but pumping sucks. Your employer should be making the transition as smooth as possible so you can balance your career and new motherhood. Look into the benefits of more family-friendly accommodations and share those with your employer. Although not federally required, this is how many workplaces eventually got family-friendly policies like paid family leave.

Demand Better

Outside of the United States, especially in Northern and Western Europe, mothers are visited in their homes by health care providers after childbirth to ensure mama and baby are healthy and well taken care of. In the Netherlands, mothers receive one week of continuous care in their homes after birth. This postpartum care includes caring for the mother, children, and even housework!

In the US, postpartum care includes a visit with your OB/GYN who will ask about your hemorrhoids six weeks after birth.

Postpartum care in the US is wildly insufficient and leaves moms to sort through issues beyond their capabilities while they adapt to the absolute mindfuck that is new motherhood.

The fundamental problem with so many programs and curriculums involving mothers is that the focus remains on the newborn or children, and the mother is largely ignored as if the kids live in a Disney movie where mothers usually don't exist. Programs like WIC (Women, Infants, and Children) are designed to help low-income women by providing some food staples like cereal and milk. If the woman is breastfeeding, they also get cheese. But still not comprehensive postpartum care.

The other huge problem with the current inadequate state of postpartum care is that care is limited to one doctor visit about six weeks after birth. The focus of that visit is two-fold—pelvic exam and a brief discussion about contraception. So many women leave the visit thinking, *well, my vagina's ok, but I'm still not.*

We desperately need comprehensive postpartum care. I would love to have those sweet Dutch people come nurture new mothers. But considering we can't even have a conversation about food stamps without someone crying, "Socialism!" let's just focus on mental health care for postpartum mothers in the spirit of compromise.

Postpartum depression is a common problem among new mothers. About one in nine moms are affected. Postpartum anxiety is also thought to be common, according to public health experts, but is also believed to be undiagnosed, so the jury's out on that one. There are many detrimental side effects to depression and anxiety in the postpartum period such as marital stress and a lack of bonding with the new addition. But the most affected, of course, is the mother.

The mother is the one trying to hide her new and frightening panic attacks from her children. She's the one unable to sleep in the few hours she has between getting up with the baby because she just can't stop worrying. She's the one whose eyes are irritated and inflamed when she's not sobbing. We need proper postpartum healthcare not just due to the side effects on the baby or the family. We need it because mothers matter.

One of the most effective ways to demand the care and treatment we need is through legislation and advocacy. There are accessible ways to improve care for mothers and point them in the right direction if postpartum depression or anxiety shows up unannounced.

In Texas, the state government implemented a Postpartum Depression Toolkit which is provided to clinicians and has comprehensive, accurate information about screening, diagnosis, and treatment of postpartum depression. With this toolkit, mothers are given information about providers in their area that treat postpartum depression and anxiety with cognitive-behavioral therapy. There's also information about coverage and reimbursement options, so hopefully, the mother doesn't avoid treatment for fear of not being able to afford it. Even if mothers begin to experience symptoms of postpartum depression or anxiety after six weeks (which is common), they'll have the tools available to help themselves.

The Texas law that sought to help provide more comprehensive postpartum care is a simple way to improve care and treatment. Look at what your representatives and senators at the state and federal level are doing to help improve conditions for mothers. If the answer is nothing, communicate with them about programs that have been effective in other states. A lot of times, lawmakers like to emulate laws similar to other states. Then, they can learn from the mistakes of other states, keeping what works and leaving out what doesn't.

Look to see which legislators are working to help conditions for mothers and do everything you can to support those efforts. For example, in Kentucky, a badass representative named Attica Scott recently proposed the Maternal Care Act, which aims to reduce maternal mortality and related emergencies.

She also gives special attention to Black women, who we know are more likely to succumb to maternal mortality. Rep. Scott focuses her bill on addressing racial bias in medicine by requiring implicit bias training, allowing patients to pay for doula services with Medicaid, and establishing a transparent panel to review maternal and infant deaths. If every state adopted a law like Rep. Scott is proposing, I do not doubt that maternal mortality rates would fall.

So many things that make motherhood difficult are beyond my control and yours. I can't make your infant sleep through the night at birth. I can't tell you how to potty train in less than twenty-four hours. I cannot make your child listen to every word you say. I can't make your labor totally painless. (Although if epidurals had a referral club, I think I'd be at the diamond level by now.)

But, as daunting as it seems, many aspects of American motherhood are senselessly difficult, and they are within our control to change. An America where so many mothers don't perish from preventable complications, where mothers have access to treatment for their postpartum depression, where having a baby doesn't completely derail a woman's career, and the division of labor is fair and manageable is within our grasp.

We need this not due to the bottom-line cost savings (although there are some) or the benefits to children and others (of which there are many). We need this for the mothers. We deserve an environment that allows us to flourish and thrive. We need to fundamentally change the way we look at issues involving the family by respecting mothers and putting more value on their needs. We're worth it.

CHAPTER SEVEN

Save Yourself, Princess

"Oh, you have the tale twisted. I am not what you thought. You had me down as a damsel. Darling, I'm the wolf."

–srwpoetry

The fairy tales, the rom-coms—they have led us astray, mamas. In the name of romance, they have taught us that a woman finally finds meaning in her life when she finds... [dramatic pause] *love.*

Women being romanticized are always in need of rescue. Cinderella needs refuge from her cruel family and mop bucket because Swiffer hadn't been invented yet, and her only hope for a new life is with her prince. Every woman in every Hallmark movie is lonely and hopeless until she meets a small-town single dad cop with a tough demeanor but a soft heart, looking for love.

In what are supposed to be large-scale romantic gestures, we're forced to witness fictional characters make terrible life decisions for the love of a mediocre white man. It is *so hard* to watch. Remember on *Boy Meets World* when Topanga works her ass off throughout high school to achieve her goal of getting into Yale *with* a scholarship? But, her high school sweetheart, Cory, doesn't want her to leave him because he's you know, an insecure high school kid. She chooses to turn down Yale in favor of the state school her Brillo-haired boyfriend could get into. In exchange for this abysmal life decision, her insecure teenage boyfriend *proposes*. They get married and live in a shitty campus apartment. The end.

These aren't romantic stories. These are cautionary tales.

Look, I'm not opposed to romance. I love love. I watch *This Is Us* every week, and I cry every other week. But romanticizing the notion that women find meaning in their lives once they find a partner is bullshit, folks.

Maybe some find meaning once they find a partner who encourages them to be the best version of themselves. Maybe finding love or making a family gives a woman the fulfillment that nothing else has because the experience helps a woman discover her purpose and value beyond being a mother or wife. It's just not the only way.

Women are perfectly capable of obtaining fulfillment outside of a romantic relationship or a family. Your partner does not need to be the primary source of fulfillment and happiness in your life. And honestly? They probably shouldn't be because that sounds exhausting.

I'm not a mental health professional, but I've read enough self-help books to know that transferring the responsibility of your worth and happiness to another person is unhealthy. Your happiness and fulfillment are no one's responsibility but your own. Often, the act of investing so much of your inner peace in someone else is a practice of codependence. So if you find yourself guilty of codependent behaviors and thinking (trust me, it's common), work to break those behaviors through cognitive-behavioral therapy, programs like Al-Anon, Brené Brown, whatever works for you, pick your poison.

Additionally, if someone close to you is guilty of codependent behavior, don't allow yourself to play into it. Set a firm boundary. Boundaries aren't a rejection of love; they can be acts of love. Don't encourage unhealthy behaviors from someone you love and care about. Plus, you already have a house full of tiny people who can't wipe their butts. You don't need to be any more needed than you are right now.

There are some easy ways to reframe your thinking about some very common codependent thoughts. Dr. Nicole LePera, also known as "The Holistic Psychologist," has an Instagram page *full* of bite-sized lessons in healing from codependency and trauma. Here are some of her ways to reframe codependent thinking into independent, healthy behavior.

+ Instead of thinking, "fix me, save me, validate my existence," think "learn me, see me, hold space for all of me."

+ Instead of being chaotic, unpredictable, or on a roller coaster of emotions, strive to be steady, safe, and show up for each other without question.

+ Instead of saying, "you complete me," say, "you enhance who I already am."

+ Instead of betraying yourself and all of your needs to receive love, do the work to meet your own needs first.

+ Instead of your relationship mirroring the pattern of your childhood experience, your relationship is based on freedom, accountability, and peace.

Isn't that beautiful? It makes me want to just let out a
"Namaste" because I am feeling very Zen right now.

You are not broken or incapable and in need of saving. No one
is a perfect being, but I'll bet you're pretty damn close. If you
have healing to do, that's something that you need to work on
for yourself and by yourself.

Think about the codependent behaviors and ways of thinking
you present. Think about the different ways you depend on
others. Explore how those behaviors make you feel. How do
you think you would feel if you no longer felt codependent or
dependent in those instances?

You're always going to depend on others in some instances. We
probably won't become so independent and so knowledgeable
that we sink the plumbing industry. As we previously
discussed, trying to do everything isn't healthy either. So, what
I want you to do is just to identify the unhealthy behaviors you
want to reframe and the things you *wish* you could do and no
longer depend on others to accomplish.

Get Your Own Toolbox

You probably think I'm going to dive into a lofty metaphor
about having the tools to take care of yourself. Nope. This
a serious suggestion and not a euphemism. I'm literally
suggesting you get your own toolbox if you don't have one
already. Whether you rent or own your home, you're no doubt
going to come across times that you'll need to fix or assemble
something, and an Allen wrench from IKEA isn't going
to cut it.

I used to stumble upon small tasks that didn't warrant hiring a contractor, but I didn't know how to do them—things like installing a curtain rod, assembling large furniture, repairing drywall, things like that. But my husband knew how, so then I would just save the tasks and ask him to do them when he had time.

UGH. I hated it. I hate asking for help, period. But I hated not knowing how to do these common household tasks. I hated staring at a curtain rod leaning against the wall because I had to wait for someone else to install it. I hated not being able to just do it myself. There's nothing in a man's DNA that gives him superior power tool skills. It's just that at some point, someone decided that he would need to learn those skills, and no one—including myself—thought I did.

It may seem minor and insignificant, and I'll agree it's not among the most important issues facing women today. But I think becoming more independent in different aspects of your life, including being handier, is an act of feminism and narrows the gap between men and women in your own life.

Through the wonder of YouTube, you can pretty much teach yourself to do anything. One of the most shocking parts of the documentary about the disastrous FYRE Festival is that one of the most pragmatic people in the operation, the pilot, actually learned to fly from playing a flight simulator on his Xbox. So, that's terrifying, but if some dude can learn to fly an entire airplane with a video game system, there's plenty of hope for you learning how to properly hammer a nail and conquer that gallery wall.

When you're starting a task for the first time, find a tutorial online and then rewatch, if necessary, while you're doing the task so you can pause when you need to. You may be shocked how simple some of these things that seemed impossible actually are once you learn to do them correctly. YouTube never judges you and your lack of home improvement skills. Go ahead and Google how to hang a picture and make sure it's level. It's fine. No shame.

If you prefer a hands-on class, check out your local hardware stores and see if they're hosting any DIY workshops. Typically stores like Home Depot host free workshops and teach you how to install tile backsplash, repair nail holes, (oh, renters, get that deposit back!), and how to properly use power tools. They also have do-it-*her*self workshops exclusively for women. Some of those workshops cover general home improvement tasks, but some are more stereotypical and Pinterest-y. But honestly, I would love to have a vertical succulent garden, so I don't hate it. Lowe's has a DIY library on their website with tutorials for everything from how to use a tape measure to how to create an accent wall with shiplap and make all your Joanna Gaines dreams come true.

The big stuff like power tools, painting supplies, etc. can be stored and shared within your household. But I would recommend having one toolbox or bag with all the essentials— hammer, wrench, screwdriver (flathead and Phillips), tape measure, and nails—that is only yours. Whether you're changing the batteries in one of your kids' toys or wanting to hang up something you just got from Home Goods, most of what you'll need is one of those basic essentials. If you have your own tools, you'll never have to dig through your partner's things trying to find what you're looking for or have to wait for someone else to find it for you. My toolbag is one of those silly ones clearly marketed for a woman because the bag and everything in it are pink. But it's honestly perfect, has everything I need, and I love it. Either buying a bag like mine or picking everything out separately at the hardware store will only cost about twenty-five dollars.

As you venture into the wild world of home improvement if you're a first-timer, as always just be kind to yourself, be willing to laugh, and accept that maybe you're not cut out for your own HGTV show just yet. I've made far too many unnecessary holes in my walls (but I know how to patch them now!), have accidentally broken things, and once broke a toe assembling an EKTORP sectional by myself. (Not recommended—that's truly a two-person job.)

Give it a shot. Step out of your comfort zone a bit and see what you can do. I think you'll be amazed by yourself and realizing what you can accomplish, all by yourself. Plus, operating power tools just makes you feel like a total badass.

Be Your Own Soulmate

> "True love ain't something you can buy yourself
> True love finally happens when you by yourself
> So if you by yourself, then go and buy yourself
> Another round from the bottle on the higher shelf."
>
> –Lizzo, "Soulmate"

Here's a little-known secret many moms know, but partners remain blissfully unaware...every Mother's Day, online moms' groups are *flooded* with disappointed moms ranting that they didn't get what they wanted from their partners.

They wanted flashy jewelry or flowers or an uninterrupted trip to Target or two hours of silence, but they didn't get it. Now they didn't ask for any of those things. But they wanted them, damnit. And they deserved them. Now they're angry.

I will not dispute that any mother deserves all the flowers and Target trips her heart desires. That's not the problem. The problem is that the angry moms are completely capable of ensuring they have the magical Mother's Days they want, but instead they're wallowing in their frustration and getting none of what they want.

First of all, if you want these things from your partner or children, tell them directly, with notice, exactly what you want. "Hey spouse, Mother's Day is coming up in two weeks. Can you please block off the afternoon because I'm planning on getting wine drunk in the bathtub and flipping through Crate & Barrel catalogs? Also, please get me a new plant. I want a monstera. Thanks. Love you." Done.

So, hopefully, your spouse will give you exactly what you want, and you'll spend your Mother's Day in a bubble bath sipping Pinot Noir instead of ranting to your local mom's group on Facebook because your spouse didn't read your mind.

Now, if your spouse or children fail at their accepted mission or you're on your own, it's time to treat yourself. Gift yourself exactly what you want. Now, I know some of us may have caviar dreams and a boxed wine budget, so clearly, no, I'm not suggesting you rack up debt so you can douse yourself in diamonds and furs and jaunt around like Moira from *Schitt's Creek*. Treat yourself in whatever capacity you can. You can treat yourself to a nap. In a mom's world, that's a luxury akin to Louis Vuitton anyway.

If you want to have a specific kind of Mother's Day, make it happen. Set your expectations and make them *known*. It's not wrong of you to want those things, it's just wrong of you to accept them not happening.

No matter your relationship status, you can love and appreciate yourself just like you want to be loved and appreciated. This is something that you should do beyond Mother's Day and special occasions. You always deserve to feel loved, and you can show that love to yourself.

You can practice this however makes the most sense for you. You may show yourself love when you take the time to peruse the floral section at Trader Joe's and pick out your favorite bouquet. You may show yourself love when you finish your makeup and take an extra moment to admire how you totally nailed that cat-eye. You may show yourself love when you toss your baggy pajama pants and old T-shirts for some cozy, matching jammies that make you feel good when you relax at night.

Instead of doing all those stereotypical things women are told to do for their partners and wait for romantic gestures in return, just cut out the middleman and do it for yourself. You don't need a partner or a special occasion to feel beautiful and confident. If wearing heels or lingerie makes you feel good, then don't just save it for date nights or wear it for your partner, do it for yourself! Prioritize how it makes *you* feel.

The lingerie industry has long flaunted models who defied physics with their towering height and waifish figures. A lingerie photoshoot was diverse if it included a woman wearing a size 0 rather than 00. The advertisements focused on the women—all with this specific aesthetic and body type—and the desire they provoked in men. The entire industry revolved around the idea of provoking sexual desire in men. If you didn't look like a Victoria's Secret model or you weren't in a heteronormative relationship, shopping for lingerie felt a bit like being a round peg trying to squeeze in a square hole.

When Rihanna, herself an objectively gorgeous woman, launched her lingerie line Savage x Fenty, it was unlike anything I had ever seen. The sizes available went up to 3X, and the models weren't hidden in a secret "plus-size" page on the website, they had a diverse group of women modeling the lingerie. As I scrolled the page, I saw women of all ethnicities and skin tones, all shapes and sizes, and they all looked stunning. For the first time I can ever recall, virtually any woman could pick out a piece of lingerie and see what it might accurately look like on her because the models actually look like her!

But representation wasn't even the most revolutionary thing about Savage x Fenty. The advertising wasn't focused on men's sexual desire. It was about making *women* feel amazing. Themes of respect, attitude, confidence, and fierceness were the focus.

It felt so novel to me, it changed the way I viewed lingerie. It's not for women of a certain size, it's for all women. It can play to a partner's sexual desire, but it doesn't have to. It's something to adorn a woman's body, so it should make the woman feel good in it, above all else.

Lizzo, who wrote the song about being your own soulmate, is a self-love superstar and often wears lingerie when she performs. That feels groundbreaking because I've never seen anyone who looks like Lizzo modeling lingerie. But there she is, wearing something you might see Beyoncé perform in, and she looks radiant, confident, and happy.

So, why can't you? It's not that lingerie isn't made for you, it is. The industry may have neglected you or got the focus all wrong. But that's their mistake. If wearing something delicate and lacy makes you feel beautiful, rock it! Do it for yourself and how it makes you feel.

Buy the flowers. Wear the lingerie. Treat yourself to the chocolate. You will be with yourself for all of your days, so show yourself some love. You should always not only practice self-love but love and treat yourself how you want to be loved and treated.

Embrace Your Weird and Wonderful Authentic Self

Being a woman in the world can be an overwhelming, exhausting, losing battle. If you're too reserved, someone will find you snobbish and cold. If you're too outspoken, someone will find you too ostentatious. If you don't have a certain level of formal education, someone will think you're uneducated in all matters. If you're an academic, someone will think you're elitist. You'll always be not enough or too much to some people.

Those are not your people.

If you're still looking, find your people. Surround yourself with people who challenge you, support you, love you, and leave you feeling happy and whole. Stop wasting your time with toxic people who are condescending and make you feel shitty. Those people who don't get you will always be out there, but you don't have to have drinks with them and invite them to your home.

Unless you're some perfect specimen like Keanu Reeves who just graces the earth to remind us that God is good, you probably have a bit of room for self-improvement. That's fine. You should pursue becoming your best self. But much of who you are is just...who you are. It's your personality. Maybe your ambition manifested in selling the most Girl Scout cookies in your troop when you were a kid, and now it manifests in you kicking ass in your career. But the ambition is a personality trait that's always been with you. There are lots of these personality traits that just make you who you are.

Instead of lamenting or taking on the futile task of trying to change these traits that are just inherently *you*, try to reframe the way you think about yourself. Maybe you're messy and not even the patron saint of organizing, Marie Kondo, could tidy your space. Maybe your sometimes-chaotic nature fuels your creativity. So take care of yourself and your place before a concerned family member nominates you for an episode of *Hoarders*, but also set realistic expectations in tune with who you know yourself to be.

Free yourself from obligation and pressure that you need to act or look a certain way, that your house must be spotless and trendy, and that you must always be the perfect mother, wife, partner, daughter, sister, employee, and friend who always put everyone's needs above her own. Do the work to be the best you *you* can be, but be *you*.

Stop allowing social media, magazines, and Instagram influencers to dictate what you should like, what you should buy, and what you should do. Ask yourself what you really want. Listen to old nineties throwbacks like Salt-N-Pepa and Ace of Base even if it makes you look ancient and totally uncool to your kids. (They're going to think you're uncool anyway.)

Choose the wall art you like instead of just what is on-trend at the moment. Make your style, your home, your life a true reflection of you.

Have a sense of humor about your quirks and be quick to laugh and dismiss them. Don't try to make yourself someone you're not. Stop setting that alarm so early when you know you're just going to hit snooze six times. You're not a morning person, it's fine. Don't allow yourself to get into character around certain people. Quit acting like you're beneath certain people and must constantly attempt to impress them—don't fumble over your words trying to find the right ones like you're talking to Meryl Streep when it's really just Ashley whose kid plays Tee-ball with yours.

We're all just fallible humans doing our best. We're not perfect. We all have quirks, flaws, and experience failure. But we're enough. We strive to be good people who try their damndest to do some good in the world and leave it a better place than when we found it. That matters, that counts. Let go of all the garbage that doesn't. Get to know your authentic self and learn to love her.

Dream On

> "I'm sick of following my dreams. I'm just going to ask them where they're goin' and hook up with them later."
>
> –Mitch Hedberg

One thing we seem to be constantly asking our children about is their dreams. What do they want to be when they grow up? What do they want the future to be like? What do they wish for? We put so much effort into facilitating their dreams even though most of us stopped dreaming a long time ago.

In Michelle Obama's brilliant memoir *Becoming*, I loved how she addressed the issue of asking children this question of what they want to be when they grow up. She said she thought asking a child what they want to be when they grow up is a completely useless question because you're asking as if growing up is a finite process: you become something, and that's it.

She rejects this notion and instead of focusing on achieving a specific goal or arriving at a certain place in life, she instead embraces the process of—hence the title—becoming. She views becoming as a constantly evolving process of pursuing a better self. She has become a powerhouse attorney, a pioneer, a nonprofit director, wife to the hunkiest president in modern history, a mother to two glorious children, the First Lady of the United States, a record-breaking author, and has done it all while somehow maintaining killer biceps.

But after earning her well-deserved place in our grandchildren's history books, she claims she is always in progress and hopes she always will be.

I always thought the question of asking a child what they wanted to be when they grew up to be a pretty useless question too. I lack the introspective brilliance Mrs. Obama possesses, so the uselessness was a bit simpler for me. How can I ask a child what they want to be when they grow up when I, a mother of two in her thirties, am not entirely sure how to answer the question myself?

That's why her perspective on "becoming" is accessible and perfect. It's daunting to choose what you want to do with your life when you've already lived much of it and are now responsible for the tiny lives in your home as well. But who do you want to become? If you were to imagine your own better self, what does she look like?

I'm not talking about superficial factors. When I ask what your better self looks like, don't immediately think *well, she's twenty-five pounds lighter and looks like Margot Robbie.* I'm talking about envisioning your better self and what her life looks like.

What is she like? Is she brave? Think about the things you can reject and remove from your life that are holding you back from fully realizing your own audacity. Is she confident? Work on affirming your strengths and acknowledging what a beautiful, incredible person you are. Is she well-educated on the issues she cares about? You've already established which issues are most important to you, so take the time to research and stay updated. Then you'll have the tools to debate a Ben Shapiro clone until he gets so flustered, he just runs away crying about the deep state.

When you imagine your better self, try to muster up the chutzpah to really dream. Think about who you always wanted to be and what you always wanted to do. If you haven't done it, do not allow yourself to wallow in grief about it or feel guilty. It is ok. In the ebbs and flows of life, dreams often fall further and further back until you forget about them, like a wilted bag of spring mix salad in the back of your refrigerator.

It is truly not too late to take a shot at your dreams. Failure is simply a part of putting yourself out there as you try to achieve something. It happens to everyone. Some of the most successful and influential people have the most epic tales of failure. J.K. Rowling was a broke, depressed, divorced single mother before she created the world of Harry Potter. Chrissy

Metz barely could put enough gas in her car to audition for *This Is Us* as she had eighty-one cents in her bank account. Some fool fired a twenty-three-year-old Oprah from her first reporting job. Sometimes it's just a humble setback, sometimes it's a nudge toward a different direction. But it's not a signal to stop what you're doing and abandon your dreams.

When I was eight years old, I used to climb a tree in my front yard and spy on the neighbors, reporting my findings in a small notebook. In my mind, I was just like aspiring writer and sleuth Harriet the Spy and not at all just some creepy, nosy kid overseeing the suburbs through binoculars. I typed my first newsletter on an ancient typewriter that my grandpa, a plumber, rescued—if memory serves correctly—from a glorified dumpster. I remember that typewriter came in a heavy, bright blue case and it must have weighed about as much as I did. I hurled it up on my bed and typed away, discarding the entire piece of paper if I made a typo.

I always wanted to be a writer, and I always wanted to write a book. It's been a dream of mine for as long as I've had dreams. Through the ebbs and flows of life, it got pushed further back. Sometimes it just seemed like an impossible dream, something you can think about, but not something that could realistically happen. Most of the time, I felt I wasn't the caliber of writer who could write and publish a book.

But then E.L. James' *Fifty Shades of Grey* topped bestseller lists all around the world and set the record for the fastest-selling paperback in the United Kingdom. If *Fifty Shades* somehow didn't make it on your to-read list, here are some lines you missed:

+ *"Welcome," he said, shoving my hair hard, "to the butt room."*

+ *Christian Grey mashed on my area with the meat of his hand. "Do you like that, you woman?"*

+ *"Do I afraid you?" Christian Grey asked, licking his eyebrow.*

It was bad—really, really bad. But imposter syndrome didn't stop ol' E.L. James from writing it, and now she's probably lounging on her yacht and doing whatever else obscenely wealthy people do like applying La Mer eye cream and avoiding paying her fair share of taxes.

If E.L. James can do it, why not me? So, finally, I decided to confront my dream, no matter how much the thought of it intimidated me. I broke it down and turned it into a goal by researching exactly what steps I needed to take. Then, I took those small steps toward my ultimate goal of writing a book and getting it published.

From the outside, it looks like a was a simple, straightforward path from book idea to publication. The path looked more like a maze full of dead-ends and rejections before I finally found my way out. I'd laugh and dismiss the people who called me crazy, and then when I was alone with my laptop, I'd think, *Oh shit, I am crazy.*

Every day, I step on Legos on the way to my laptop to write. I answer questions about why we have belly buttons and hear the chorus of *"Mommmmmmmmmmmmmy"* from my two kids all day because you know who doesn't care about deadlines? Kids. They're here to keep you humble and ask for snacks.

But right now you are reading my dream realized. It felt daunting in the beginning, and honestly, most of the time it still does as I occasionally allow myself to be overwhelmed with the feeling of being so close to achieving a lifelong dream. The odds were against me, but it wasn't impossible. I knew there was a chance I could be successful, and I just wanted to shoot my shot, be able to tell myself I really tried to achieve this dream and not just leave it to haunt me. I pushed through failures and setbacks and damnit, I did it!

Whatever you want to do, whatever dream you want to achieve, there's someone out there who is so much worse than you, but did it. Do you have a dream of being an attorney? Let me remind you that Kellyanne Conway, Michael Cohen, and Rudy Giuliani all got through law school, passed the bar, and, at this writing, only one of them is in federal prison. Want to run for political office? There are men in office right now half as intelligent as you who have probably been in Congress longer than you've been alive. Do you want to be president of the United States? Recent history has proven anyone can be president and perhaps we even took that a bit too far, but hey! Now the bar is so low, you best be careful not to trip on it. You are capable and worthy of accomplishing your dreams just as much as anyone else.

Before You Save the World, Save Yourself

After a discussion with Nelson Mandela, Oprah Winfrey had the idea to found a school in Mandela's home of South Africa. She wanted to help girls who grew up much like Oprah herself, "economically disadvantaged, but not poor in mind or spirit." The school, Oprah Winfrey Leadership Academy for

Girls, provides quality education to hundreds of talented girls each year.

Mandela himself had the opportunity to see Oprah's gift in action and said, "When I went to the opening of her school, I looked at the shining faces of these young women and thought every one of them has the potential to be an Oprah Winfrey."

Since the school opened in 2007, Oprah said every girl who has graduated from the school and gone forward to college has had the same fundamental goal—to become a leader in her own life. Oprah teaches a class each year, called (seriously) "Life 101" and regarding each class of little budding future Oprahs itching to make a difference, she says:

"Can she save the world? Well, I teach them first: save yourself. It is your job to make yourself whole, not perfect, but whole and full. Your real work in life is to fill yourself 'til your cup runneth over so that you're never grasping and needy, clamoring, and insecure."

As you explore new opportunities in activism and discover your role in making our world a better place, you must save yourself first.

CHAPTER EIGHT

Dad's Not Babysitting

"Women will only have true equality when men share with them the responsibility of bringing up the next generation."

–Ruth Bader Ginsburg

I'm generally quick to politely smile and nod at the cliché comments I, like most moms, get such as, "Oh, you certainly have your hands full" when checking out at the grocery while the smallest kid is having a meltdown because I didn't get the pink unicorn sprinkle Pop-Tarts she wanted. Over the years I've been a mom, I've gotten used to the comments and imagine they're the stay-at-home mom equivalent to a coworker shooting finger guns at your cubicle and shouting, "Hey, working hard or hardly working?"

But the one comment I cannot bear to dismiss is, "Oh, is your husband babysitting today?" when I'm spotted out without my kids.

I'm sorry, is he—what? …*Babysitting?* No, he's parenting. I never took a paternity test, but based on that one's head circumference at birth and that one's sarcasm, I'm pretty sure they're his.

I hate this question because it assumes the majority of childrearing responsibility falls to the mother, so much so that the father in a heteronormative relationship gets no more credit in raising the child than a teenage babysitter who watches the kid every other weekend would. It places undue pressure on the mother to shoulder the entire weight of childbearing and it's extremely offensive to a father, who is every bit as much of a parent as she is.

The crux of the issue is that exactly—the father is every bit of a parent a mother is.

There's this idea that mothers are born nurturers and are innately better suited for parenting that has significantly influenced our society and even our lives today. Mothers in the American Revolution raised their sons to be revolutionaries and war heroes and their daughters to be wives and mothers. Hundreds of years later, many of us are still grappling with the societal pressure of the men to be providers and the women to be mothers.

The idea of mothers being born nurturers and thus the natural choice to take on a primary parenting role has been present for…well, possibly ever. The revered Virgin Mary is an omnipresent symbol of this idea in many Christian religions. The religious influence on this way of thinking is still influential. If you investigate whether or not mothers are inherently nurturing more so than fathers, you'll find many affirming opinions, and they'll all be from religious sources such as the Mormon Church.

The truth is that the idea that mothers are just more naturally suited for the nurturing role necessary of a parent is a myth. We've been perpetuating it for centuries, but it's not based in fact and there's no actual psychological evidence to support it.

There is a natural, biological response mothers experience. They have the ability to birth babies, which, *hello*, is amazing. When their babies cry or are held close, a mother will likely feel the milk let down in her breasts so she can feed her baby. It's an absolute marvel of biology and it still absolutely amazes me to consider that so many of us mothers share that common experience.

But does it make us better parents than our partners or mothers who did not biologically give birth to their children? Nope.

The maternal instinct that a mother inherently knows best how to take care of her children is not real. The feeling of unadulterated horror you may have felt when you held your baby for the first time and thought, *Oh shit, are they going to expect me to take this home? That's* real. That's normal. It's not that your maternal instinct hadn't kicked in yet; you never had one. None of us do.

Now, that does not mean you:

+ Did not want to become a mother.

+ Do not love your children.

You don't have to have an internal, superhuman ability to care for your children to want to become a mother, and you are a stellar mom who loves her children. I have never experienced love like the love I have for my children. I feel like my heart has been stretched until the limits cease to be. I still sneak into their rooms at night and kiss their sweet little faces and thank God for blessing my life with them. And then I thank God they're sleeping because I am *so* freaking tired.

When your children run to you crying for comfort when they scraped a knee or jump up and down in excitement when you pick them up from school, that's just because they genuinely love you. It's all you. It's not something you were born with or a gene that was magically activated when you became a mother; the love and bond you have with your children is something you have cultivated.

Mothers often shift into the primary parenting role or stay at home while the other parent works outside the home, but again, this isn't because mothers are just naturally the best fit for the role. It may be the result of gender stereotypes or cultural norms. It may be (and should be) an individual choice. It may be just a practical decision as the combination of a lack of family leave, the gender pay gap, and the astronomical cost of childcare makes the mother staying at home with the children the soundest financial decision.

If circumstances had changed and it made equal logistical sense for the father to stay at home and both parents agreed it was best for their individual needs, then that makes just as much sense as the mother staying home. The barriers that make this scenario less likely, socially constructed or otherwise, shouldn't exist anyway.

Unlike other forms of systemic misogyny that are so deeply ingrained in our culture, shifting men to supporting roles in parenting hurts both women and men.

Mothers are expected to feel honored when they're treated as a superior parent. *No one can do it like moms! Moms are just so good at it. Gosh, I could never do what they do.* The truth is moms do it because they have to. Some partners are perfectly happy with the arrangement of mothers taking the brunt of parenting duties. But to refuse necessary parenting duties like diaper changing just because you're a man is—pun intended—shitty.

I like to think poo-phobic fathers are the minority. I think most fathers genuinely want to be just as involved as mothers in parenting. But our society does not make it easy for them. I can't tell you how many times I watched my husband dejectedly return to our table at a restaurant because the men's restroom didn't have a changing table.

If we want equality in our lives, we have to promote equality in coparenting.

Don't Let Toxic Masculinity Infect Your Family

Modern fatherhood has been infiltrated by toxic masculinity and it's not just simply a refusal to change diapers; it's a cultural burden that affects the whole family. Toxic masculinity puts boys and men in a box that restricts the way they express themselves. Instead of expressing a wide range of emotions—happiness, sadness, disappointment—like you know, humans do, men are limited to an "alpha male" role. Instead of being sensitive and affectionate, they stick to more stereotypical gender expressions like anger. Aloof, angry, alpha male—not exactly the ideal coparenting partner.

The alpha male has become an unattainable goal for some men who aspire to be strong, attractive, confident, bold—a man's man who gets things done. Think John Wayne strutting around the Old West ready to draw his pistol at any moment. It's mostly a completely fictional concept. When I looked up modern examples of an alpha male, I found a slideshow of actor Ryan Reynolds. In one pic, he stares intensely into the camera, in another, his jacket is agape exposing his chiseled chest, in another, he's sporting a beard and a suit. I looked at all of them... You know, for research.

But the real Ryan Reynolds beyond the muscle-bound slideshow doesn't buy into the alpha male father bullshit. During an appearance on *Late Night with Seth Meyers*, Meyers asked Reynolds for some advice as he was expecting his first child. Of all the parenting advice and new baby tips he could espouse, he instead advised Meyers to focus on his wife and what she needs.

"Just do the dirty work, man," Reynolds said. "You gotta do the diapers, you gotta do the middle of the night thing. I mean, your wife—a human being will exit your wife, so she's done enough. Just change the diapers and do all that stuff."

Hell yes, do the dirty work. Even his goddess wife Blake Lively didn't get an exemption to the tribulation of labor and childbirth. She probably even wore those gigantic mesh undies the nurses give you in the hospital! She deserves to have her chiseled hunk of a husband tend to their baby while she gets a damn break.

Toxic masculinity teaches men that anything typically associated with women is weak and to be avoided. So in fatherhood, that means shutting off emotional responses and avoiding being too affectionate, too sensitive. But possessing emotions doesn't make you weak. Ignoring your true feelings is weak.

What takes real strength is to reject toxic masculinity and embrace your true feelings. Confronting emotions and expressing them in a healthy, constructive way isn't always easy. It takes a strong person to take inventory of how they're feeling and be open and honest about their emotions. In a society that senselessly teaches men to be detached, it's a real act of courage to be sensitive and loving.

Men are not unfeeling creatures. Do not buy into the false narrative that men are just wired differently and they just don't feel the same emotions that women do—it's not true. Talk to the men in your life about their feelings; ask them what they're thinking and if it's difficult for them to open up—acknowledge that. Thank them for trusting you with their feelings.

We have to break this cycle and raise our sons better, so they'll one day grow up to be good men. Toxic masculinity is a cancer placed upon young boys. It devalues and disparages women. It teaches men—who are human beings—to bury and reject emotion. It's an exercise in cruelty and injustice to allow men to believe that their emotions are unnatural and should be rejected.

Outside of harm to men and their families, the principles of toxic masculinity harm our entire society in devastating ways from contributing to rape culture to influencing intimate partner violence. As mothers and feminists, we have a moral obligation to do what we can to stop the oppression of future generations of women. How we raise our sons is a powerful way we can do our part to change the future for women.

Teach your sons about ways to express their feelings as early as possible. The ultimate example of nontoxic masculinity, and where Mister Rogers' legacy lives on, is the cartoon spinoff, *Daniel Tiger's Neighborhood* where Daniel Tiger teaches fantastic lessons on dealing with emotions. I think this is a great example because there is no burying or ignoring emotions—definitely, no "boys don't cry" narratives. Emotions are welcome, but children need the tools to regulate their emotions and deal with them in a healthy way. For example, Daniel talks about taking deep breaths and asking for help instead of getting frustrated and launching a toy at your mom's head. Honestly, most adults could probably benefit from a little moment of Zen from Daniel Tiger, too.

Don't allow gender roles to restrict your son's activities. If your son has as interest in playing with dolls, encourage that! Maybe he wants to pretend to be a dad, so play like a dad—rock the baby and change the diapers. Teach them that these are the things that dads do.

Be affectionate and loving with your sons. Talk to them about their days and dig into how things make them feel while encouraging that you're a safe place to talk about anything. Normalize expressing emotions and reinforce healthy ways to manage them. (It's hard when you're a kid!) Tell them that boys *cry*. Never dismiss their feelings or ask them to brush them off; if they're willing to open up about how they feel, let them know you'll always listen.

As we reject toxic masculinity within our coparenting relationships and with our children, we're promoting a household that deals with emotions in a healthy, productive way. We all have feelings. None of us should be hiding them. Instead, we just need to work on ways to express ourselves that don't cause any harm and encourage an environment that is always a safe place for conveying our feelings.

There's a tired trope that feminists hate men simply because feminists are quick to point out issues that exist involving men. So, let me be clear—rejecting toxic masculinity is an act of love. We do not hate men. We have men in our lives who we *love*, and we want to liberate them from this fictional pressure that is holding them back from being their authentic, loving selves.

In the *Will to Change: Men, Masculinity, and Love*, feminist icon bell hooks emphasized that both women and men have not historically done a great job of encouraging men to love and this is something we must change.

> "To create loving men, we must love males. Loving maleness is different from praising and rewarding males for living up to sexist-defined notions of male identity. Caring about men because of what they do for us is not the same as loving males for simply being. In patriarchal culture, males are not allowed simply to be who they are and to glory in their unique identity. Their value is always determined by what they do. In an anti-patriarchal culture, males do not have to prove their value and worth. They know from birth that simply being gives them value, the right to be cherished and loved."
>
> -bell hooks, *Will to Change: Men, Masculinity, and Love*

We must show the men in our lives, who were not taught from birth that they have the inherent value and right to be cherished and loved, that they were lied to, but we are here to help them heal. We must cherish and love our sons and do our best to keep them close to that harmonious wholeness they were both with.

Let's show the males in our lives that we know and appreciate their worth. Let's help them reject the constraints of toxic masculinity and encourage them to share their hearts.

Balance the Parenting Scales

In a relationship with a woman who biologically births the babies, the other partner—no matter how much they kick ass and desire to be involved—defaults to a supporting role in many aspects.

I know when I hit around hour forty-two of labor, I started giving my husband the stink eye. I thought, *damn. Let's tag out. I'll stand on the side of the bed and tell you when to breathe because that Lamaze shit isn't cutting it right now.* Ooo! Or those nights at 4:30 a.m., when the newborn baby started crying again for the twenty-third time that night, and I just took a moment to pause and admire my husband soundly sleeping with his worthless nipples.

No matter how wonderful your partner is, there are realistic limits to what they can do and how they can help. They can't birth babies like Arnold Schwarzenegger in that horrifying bad nineties flick *Junior*. Their nipples are going to remain worthless. Even worse, our world does not make it easy for both parents to be equally involved. On the micro level at home, you have some control over how involved your partner can be. On the macro level, you have a lot less control and your kid may be well out of diapers before there's change, but you're not helpless and things are not hopeless.

At home, even if your partner is driven into a supporting role, there are still ways they can be involved. During pregnancy, labor, and childbirth, that is the time for your partner to treat you like an absolute goddess. You're creating life so your partner can create some brownies in the kitchen if a craving hits. Your partner can shift into the supporting role and do everything in their power to make you as comfortable as possible. This is the time to show their appreciation for what you're doing for your collective family and inundate you with love.

Their nipples may be worthless, but your partner is not. Breastfeeding is extremely hard, draining work, especially while recovering from a major medical ordeal. So, again, your

partner needs to shift into a supporting role. If you choose
to breastfeed and are responsible for your baby's nutrition,
your partner can step it up in other areas. For example, when
I was nursing, my husband changed nearly all the diapers.
Arrangements like that help balance an otherwise naturally
unequal situation. Also, if you're nursing, you're probably
ravenous all the time, so your partner can fetch you a water
bottle, some healthy snacks, and a book to make it a comfier
experience for you.

The biological limitations like childbirth and breastfeeding are
pretty much the only unmovable barriers to a complete balance
of parenting responsibilities. For example, if you're formula-
feeding instead of breastfeeding, there's no reason a partner
can't take on 50 percent of the feedings. You're wonderful, but
we've already established that you don't possess a superhuman
maternal instinct that makes you the superior parent. So, let's
work to achieve a balance.

I'm not naïve in thinking that, beyond biological factors,
you can achieve perfect balance in parenting and that there
aren't more factors that are imbalanced beyond your control.
I'll get to the unbalanced barriers that stand in the way on a
macro level in just a bit. There's no magical formula or advice
I can give to help every mother achieve perfect balance in
their households. I cannot begin to understand the multitude
of factors in your life that create an imbalance, and I will
not pretend to. Furthermore, I understand much of this
conversation is one of privilege and there may be single moms
reading this thinking, *"Oh, boo hoo, your partners aren't
changing enough diapers."* I see you all, and your struggles
deserve to be addressed too.

This is an extremely individual issue, and there's no one-size-fits-all solution. So, what you need to do if you're in a coparenting relationship is to examine it for areas of imbalance and think about if you're ok with it. There are always going to be imbalances, but if neither parent has a problem, there's no problem. It's about what works for you. On nights that I'm not scouring the junk drawer for take-out menus, I love to cook. So, I don't want to divide the cooking responsibilities in half. That's what works for us, and in our circumstance, that's what matters.

The imbalances you need to be aware of are the parenting roles you may tend to fall into. Is one parent always the disciplinarian? Is one parent always the fun one? Are the kids seeing only one parent doing most of the household duties? Is one parent overwhelmed with obligations that are only noticed if they don't get done? Those are the areas to pay extra attention to and discuss redistributing.

Just keep an open and honest dialogue with your partner while remaining respectful and kind. Sometimes, conversations about imbalance will be mundane discussions about fairly dividing household chores no one wants to do. Sometimes, you'll encourage your partner to go take the kids out for ice cream or have some time to themselves. Whether or not you're committed to a romantic relationship or have split and are navigating coparenting, you've scrambled your eggs with this person. If they're going to continue to have a role in your children's lives, everyone should maintain as fair of a balance as possible.

Some things are less in your control because equal parenting roles aren't the norm. That's when you need to influence change on a macro level. Mothers are constantly assumed to take on the majority of the parenting responsibilities. For fathers who want to be equally involved, it's not always easy.

Every time a father joins a playdate, the group of moms tends to act like they're suddenly involved in a live episode of *To Catch a Predator*. There's a lot of pressure on stay-at-home moms, but I think stay-at-home dads feel the heat a bit more as they grapple with the typical demands of parenting and the societal demands that try to keep dads within their stereotypical gender roles.

Normalize involved dads. Talk to your mom friends about how involved your partner is and how you strive to maintain equal parenting roles. Ask the dads that show up in playgroups about their kids' sleep cycles, how much you all hate *Caillou*, and all the other silly things you talk to the moms about. Recognize that being a very involved dad can come with challenges and do what you can to make things more comfortable.

When you identify other challenges dads face, start a conversation with the people who have the power to change it. Changing tables should be readily available in both women's *and* men's restrooms. When you see this, bring it to a manager or owner's attention and let them know that men change diapers too, so please consider installing a table in their restroom. If a company provides maternity leave, but not family leave, let them know that it's vital for all parents to have time to bond with their new children and to please consider adopting a more inclusive policy. Sometimes all it takes is asking. Be respectful, polite, and friendly. Sometimes results only happen with further escalation (like *more* asking, petitions, etc.), but at least the issue is brought to their attention, and now they're aware of the problem.

My husband may not consider it one of his top career accomplishments, but his persistence in getting a changing table was one time I've been proudest. He worked in an outpatient counseling center. Most of his clients were men, and some of them were new fathers. To make it a bit easier for them to get to therapy, they'd bring their babies along. But, like many predominantly male spaces, there wasn't a changing table.

So, my husband requested a changing table and because he works for the federal government, this was quite a task. The request mystified many as a changing table isn't a common request; in fact, it probably hadn't been requested anywhere before. But he persisted, and after several months, his clients had a safe, clean, quiet place to change their babies.

It was just a changing table. But now, every parent who enters has what they need to take care of their babies while they take care of themselves. It empowers fathers to know that they're supported and deserve equal access.

These seem like small things and small conversations. But they can make a big impact. Stepping outside stereotypical gender roles is brand new information for some people, and when you have these conversations, you're normalizing equality in parenting. Equality is equality, and when we balance the scales and equalize parenting, we all benefit.

Fight for Equal Rights

An embodiment of gender equality, Justice Ruth Bader Ginsburg made groundbreaking strides in defeating gender discrimination with one simple strategy—she focused on discrimination against men. During a time when she was

discriminated against for daring to be a woman with legal
aspirations and she was well aware of the prejudice women
encountered in their daily lives, she took on the cases of
a man who was denied a caregiver's tax credit (Moritz v.
Commissioner) and a man who would have to send his
girlfriend to buy him a beer because the law allowed women
under twenty-one to purchase alcohol, but not men (Craig
v. Boren).

Because Justice Ginsburg was a phenomenal attorney,
relentless worker, and argued her cases flawlessly, she won.
But, because she's brilliant, she also knew these cases were
not simply about tax credits and beer. The success of these
cases struck down laws and practices discriminating based on
sex immediately and set precedent for women and men to be
treated equally in the eyes of the law in countless areas.

Craig v. Boren was the first case using an intermediate
scrutiny test applied to equal protection and discrimination
constitutional challenges. In a snowball effect, it started with
men being discriminated against in Oklahoma, but then
resulted in allowing women in the previously male-only
Virginia Military Institute (United States v. Virginia) and that
firing a transgender employee was a form of sex discrimination
(Glenn v. Brumby). The Craig v. Boren precedent was used in
countless instances of gender discrimination.

Years after Justice Ginsburg delivered the opinion of United
States v. Virginia, she reflected on the legacy of striking down
gender discrimination and the inclusion of women in the
military and military institutions. "There's a brigadier general
in the Marines, and she's in charge of manpower," she said, "I
just love that."

Justice Ginsburg understood decades ago that the fight for equal rights for women must include men. By fighting for equal rights for men, women indirectly gained equal rights in other areas. So, often in advocating for equality for men's issues, it benefits our self-interest as well.

But, of course, it's more than that. Discrimination against men is wrong, just as discrimination against women or any other group is wrong. If we're going to take a stand against injustice and demand equal rights, it needs to be across the board.

It's tricky to discuss discrimination against men sometimes because there is a great deal of ugliness in some social movements advocating for the rights of men. Some "men's rights" groups have an androcentric philosophy that marginalizes women and promotes misogyny. Some of the issues they seek to resolve aren't quite the injustices they proclaim. I believed the myth that there was a gender bias in family court against fathers until I couldn't find any evidence to support it. Men's rights groups have been associated with opposing the criminalization of marital rape, advocating for the opportunity to decline paternity rights and responsibilities, and general anti-feminist assholery. So, when I talk about issues that affect men and fathers, I am not talking about hopping in a picket line with oppressive men's rights groups.

Men's rights groups do themselves a great disservice by dabbling in falsehoods and misogyny because several of the issues they concern themselves with do have truth to them. For example, we have a devastatingly high firearm suicide rate in the United States, and 86 percent of firearm suicide victims are men. In late 2019, the Trump administration proposed a rule to roll back Obama-era protections and allow adoption agencies to discriminate based on sexual orientation, prohibiting same-sex couples from providing loving homes to children in need of them. These are real issues that affect men and fathers.

We need to be aware of inequity facing fathers just as we're aware of the injustices mothers face. Fighting for equality in fatherhood also advances equality for women. As Justice Ginsburg said, we will have true equality only when we fully share the responsibility of raising the next generation. Men of quality support women's equality, so let's support the men in our lives and work together toward true equality for all.

PART III

Role Modeling

CHAPTER NINE

Be the Village

A t a Pride parade in Austin, Texas, as members of the
LGBTQ+ community and allies marched down the street
waving flags and wearing their finest rainbow-colored attire,
many stopped in their tracks to a foreign sight that brought
them to instant tears.

A small local church had gathered on the sidelines—also in
their finest rainbow attire—grasping signs and wearing T-shirts
that said, "Free Mom Hugs," "Free Dad Hugs," and "Free
Pastor Hugs." Marchers in the parade would read the signs and
T-shirts and run as fast as they could into the arms of a stranger
there only to give them love.

Jen Hatmaker, mother, bestselling author, and evangelical
church leader posted a photo of herself glowing with love and
firmly grasping a young man sporting a rainbow bandana. She
said their arms were never empty, and as they told attendees
they were impossibly loved, needed, and precious, they heard
things like: "I miss this," "My mom doesn't love me anymore,"
"My Dad hasn't spoken to me in three years," and a pleading,
"Please, just one more hug."

The church was inspired to show love to the LGBTQ
community with literal open arms by Sara Cunningham,

founder of Free Mom Hugs. Cunningham is a Christian mom
of a gay son who formed the group of affirming parents and
allies who seek to cover the LGBTQ community with the
unconditional love only parents can give. They educate families
as well as church and civic leaders about LGBTQ issues
and encourage them to celebrate and love the community
as they do.

Cunningham said of the Free Mom Hugs movement, "If I don't
fight for my son (and his rights) like my hair is on fire, then
who will?"

Well, now, gratefully, her movement has spread to chapters in
nearly every state, and we can answer Cunningham's question:
Jen Hatmaker will. Evangelical pastors will. I will. Hundreds of
parents all over the country will.

Hatmaker is a perfect role model for what it means to be the
village. She's a cisgender ally married to a man. Driven by
the same faith some use to discriminate; she believes that the
LGBTQ community is deserving of love and civil rights. She's
gained a huge following for being a lovable, relatable mom who
shares funny photos and heartwarming anecdotes. But she built
much of her career writing books with Christian publishers and
headlining speaking tours with audiences of Christian women.
The evangelical market has been her bread and butter.

So when she followed her conviction and heart supporting the
LGBTQ community and unequivocally stated that she supports
same-sex marriage and believes LGBTQ relationships can be
holy, it was a bold statement that came with real consequences.
LifeWay Christian Stores, at the time a mega Southern Baptist
bookseller and the publisher of one of Hatmaker's bestselling
books, announced they would discontinue selling her Bible
studies and books. Her formerly devoted fans mailed her

books—with burned pages—back to her home address. She began receiving death threats.

But she never backed down. Instead of launching into a damage control campaign and trying to save her base, she doubled down on her support of the LGBTQ community, Black Lives Matter, refugees, and voiced her disappointment and opposition to the presidential campaign of a sexual predator. When pressure continued to mount for her to apologize, she posted an image of herself with her signature huge earrings, an even bigger smile, flip-flops, and a black tank with the words "I ain't sorry" across the chest. The caption just read, "Mood." And damn, if it isn't.

Hatmaker continued to rise above the vitriol and hatred. She may have sacrificed some fans and career opportunities, but she never sacrificed her principles. She never backed down from supporting the communities she knew deserved support. Her empire grew and expanded while Lifeway closed every brick and mortar store it operated.

The spirit of the proverb "it takes a village to raise a child" is not that the community is responsible for raising children, but that the entire community must be involved in promoting a happy, healthy environment for children to thrive. The community should always look out for children and support parents.

Too often, parents or the children themselves are left to fight their own battles and advocate for themselves without the community support. Parenting is hard, and sometimes we're all just treading water, but these moments make me wonder *where is the village?* When someone needs support, shouldn't we jump in?

We should jump in with our passion for what is right, our conviction that we're doing the right thing, and our refusal to back down. This is exactly what Jen Hatmaker did and continues to do. It couldn't have been easy for her, and she suffered real consequences for speaking out, but she never backed down. Be willing to take a stand for what is right even if it means stepping out of line and making some sacrifices. There are parents and children in your community who are wondering where their village is. It's time to open your arms and heart for them.

Support Parents

#TrayvonMartin
#JordanDavis
#EricGarner
#JohnCrawford
#MichaelBrown
#TamirRice
#AntonSterling
#PhilandoCastile
#BreonnaTaylor
#GeorgeFloyd

For some mothers, it seemed like there was always a new hashtag trending, signifying yet another Black life senselessly lost—usually a young Black man, sometimes even a child. Often killed by a police officer. Unarmed. Justice denied. And then these mothers would look into the eyes of their precious Black baby boys and feel unnerving, crushing fear.

I was fortunate enough to hear a young Black mother voice these concerns directly, so I had no excuse not to listen. She said she was terrified of raising a Black child in this age of unjust killings, and her child was only a baby in diapers. She spoke about how she and her husband pray for his protection and their awareness of the lessons they'll need to teach him. Lessons like keeping his hands out of his pockets in stores, what language to use when stopped by the police, and what places aren't safe for him to be due to the color of his skin.

She urged her friends to speak out, especially the white ones. She warned them that when they admire her cute little family and coo over her young son, to consider that they might be next.

That got my attention. I felt so foolish and ashamed when I thought of the concerns I had for my children: *Are we saving enough for college? How will I help them heal a broken heart? How can I help their hurt feelings?* I'm a neurotic mom. I have plenty of worries. But I never worried about my kids becoming a hashtag.

Sometimes, parents need support, and they usually aren't as direct and forthcoming about their needs. When a mom is being open enough to share her justified fear of the future for her son, we need to listen. We need to be in the village for her.

To be the village in those situations, we can't be too afraid to say Black Lives Matter. We need to be bold enough to push back on those who claim it's offensive and tell them how offensive we find it that innocent Black lives are lost unjustly. We need to practice anti-racism in ourselves and call out racism when we see it. We need to teach our children about the injustices of the world and how to break the cycle of bigotry. When someone who is facing injustice asks us to take a stand and speak out, we need to oblige, especially if we're coming from a place of privilege, making it even easier for us to do so.

Sometimes a mom in need of her village doesn't shout out that she needs help—it sounds more like a whisper. We need to be on the lookout for the ones who need support. Sometimes it's the strong ones who always seem to be headed in three different directions and balance all the demands of their lives with a smile. Encourage these moms to stop a minute, breathe, and ask how they're *really* doing. Maybe they're doing fantastic. Maybe they're on the verge of a nervous breakdown. But you won't know, and you won't be able to support them if they need it unless you ask and build a relationship that allows them to understand that you're a kind, nonjudgmental, safe person to turn to if they need some help or a hug.

When you're standing in solidarity with Black moms and people of color as a white person, know your place. You are a guest in their space. Do not burden them with your pain and discomfort in a difficult time; it's not fair for them to carry your load on top of their own insurmountable anguish. If you're at a Black Lives Matter protest, for example, as a white person, you should not lead chants or bring the attention to yourself. You should stand in solidarity however the Black leaders, who have been doing this work for so long, deem it best. Protect them with your privilege. Be quiet. Learn. Listen.

All moms carry so much and keep their battles hidden. There are incredibly sad, life-altering events we all endure as moms, and society pressures us to keep it private. Miscarriage is very common, with up to 25 percent of pregnancies affected. Traditionally, women are advised to hold off on announcing pregnancies until they reach the second trimester and the risk of miscarrying significantly drops.

I don't think waiting to speak of a pregnancy until twelve weeks' gestation should be the accepted standard for *every* expectant woman. Again, like most parenting decisions, it's extremely personal. If a mother is very private, she can conceal her pregnancy for nine months like Kylie Jenner, and that is her choice.

But, as soon as a line pops up on that pregnancy test, I'll squeal with excitement and be ready to celebrate if the mom is celebrating. If she happens to be the one in four pregnancies that end in miscarriage, and she doesn't want to be alone, then I'll be there to listen and grieve along with her. Whether a mom is celebrating advancing a healthy pregnancy or mourning a loss, she deserves to feel supported and loved during that time. If she finds comfort in the support of others, I hate to think she should be denied that just because societal norms dictate she shouldn't share.

If a mom shares that she lost her pregnancy, she deserves at least the same amount of love and support she received when she announced the news that she was pregnant. As the village, we shouldn't allow any discomfort with the news to distract from supporting someone in mourning.

Moms need their village so they can better support themselves and their kids. Look for the moms who show signs of struggle. Always be sure to lock eyes and smile at them, ask them how they're doing, be there to listen, and show them some compassion. Maybe they need some help and just don't know which resources are available, but you do. Maybe they're grappling with their child's recent autism diagnosis and you happen to know about an awesome local group of parents who specialize in autism resources and support. Maybe they're dealing with depression and you can share your therapist's number and experience of getting help. Maybe they just needed someone to recognize them and ask how they're doing because they need a reminder that they matter.

Being the village sometimes means showing up and standing up for what is right alongside courageous moms who are trying to do right by their kids. Some of the issues parents and children face are best solved by some type of systemic change, and that is not an easy task; it's definitely not a small undertaking for one person.

If a mom is standing up for the rights of her child, have her back. It's maddening to see the source of outrage from issues like kids using the bathrooms of their identified gender and racist dress codes that police traditional Black hairstyles. Most of the time, it's not the kids in the schools who would be directly affected by expressing their outrage. They generally are too consumed with their own teenage lives to read their school's handbook or notice which students are using which bathrooms. The kids don't mind. The people who are having shouting matches in school board meetings and defending established oppressive practices in the name of moral outrage? It's the parents.

How discouraging it must be to fight for the rights of your child and learn that your adversaries are fellow parents. Don't be one of those parents making another parent's already trying job more difficult.

If you learn of a difficult situation brewing, take action at the earliest possible moment. If it's something your child is already aware of, talk to them about advocating for their fellow students, looking out for signs of bullying, and showing students affected a little extra kindness. If the parent involved is ready to take action in advocating for the right of their child, let them know they have your full support. There's strength in numbers for advocacy, so be willing to show support at school board meetings, write a letter to the editor of your local paper, or whatever is needed at that moment to make a difference.

You'll find struggling moms everywhere you go. You'll see them trying to deescalate a tantrum at Target. You'll see them wearing their house slippers running their kid to school, late. Again. You'll see them forget sunscreen at the pool. You've been this mom. You are this mom. These little not-so-Instagram-worthy moments of parenting are much easier to endure when you run into a fellow mom willing to smile, lend a hand (or some sunscreen), and just say "Hey, you're doing a great job."

All around us are moms coping with invisible struggles. They may be struggling with their health, marriage, career, finances, family, who knows? But none of us know all the idiosyncrasies of anyone's life but our own. So always meet moms with compassion as if they're fighting a battle you can't see.

Support Kids

What made Pride parade participants run into the arms of strangers was a history of heartbreaking abandonment. I cannot fathom abandoning the child you raised simply because they opened up about who they really are.

I encourage others not to judge parents for the decisions they make, but I'm having a hard time not judging the hell out of a parent who abandoned their child because they were born on the LGBTQ spectrum. Parenting isn't about coddling or shielding your child from the consequences of the decisions they make. You don't have to agree with or love every single thing they do. (I can't imagine my mother loved my pink hair and Hot Topic-chic clothing I wore in high school.) You should love them for who they are. Being LGBTQ is not a choice any more than eye color is a choice. But abandoning them is a choice and not one any parent has any excuse to make.

Yet, we know this happens. Children are placed in impossible situations all the time by the cruel decisions of adults. As the grown-ups in these situations, we need to confront them head-on and not leave children to navigate cruel policies and unnecessary injustices.

Have you seen those heartwarming stories being circulated on social media about a sweet first-grader who made and sold hundreds of keychains so he could use the money raised to pay off other students' lunch debt at his school? The articles detailing his motivations with photos of an adorable, toothless child grasping a giant check have been shared thousands of times by people pleased that the kids are all right.

Sure, the kids may be all right in their selfless acts of kindness. But the adults are not all right. Lunch debt?! We're celebrating some small kid's foray into child labor so he could release his classmates from the lunchtime debtor's prison of peanut butter and shame sandwiches? Kudos to this kind kid, but this isn't just a feel-good story, this is a dystopian nightmare.

Lunch at school is a necessary part of every kid's day. Imagine how grumpy you would be if you were forced to skip lunch and how difficult you would find focusing on your tasks. I've seen what the intermittent fasting fad has done to women, so I know you'd be grouchy. If children are facing food insecurity at home, school lunch is even more vital as it may be the only balanced meal they get all day.

When children don't have the funds to pay, schools have to decide on how to proceed. (The easy decision would be, uh, to feed them. They're just kids, for fuck's sake.) Many schools have come up with an alternative lunch for kids who can't pay, like a cold cheese sandwich instead of the hot lunch all the other kids are eating. They stamp kids' hands with "I need lunch money." They ban them from participating in extracurricular activities. These actions are used to embarrass and shame children, who surely have no way to pay, into resolving their lunch debt.

One school district even sent letters home to parents whose children owed more than ten dollars in lunch debt and warned them that if the debt was not paid, their children could be put in foster care. The school employee who wrote the threatening letters, which were sent to dozens of families, scolded families for not providing their children with breakfast or lunch and warned they would be "reported to the proper authorities" if not resolved. The local county manager had to reassure parents that the foster system is not intended to terrorize them into paying lunch debt, and they have no intention of ever removing a child from their home due to not paying a lunch bill.

The ones suffering the most from the lunch debt debacle are, of course, the children. Even families who qualify for free or reduced lunch often can accrue lunch debt if their application is delayed or otherwise caught up in the bureaucratic process. So even parents who have demonstrated financial need may have children with lunch debt. But the children affected should not be held responsible for their inability to pay, but they're the ones going hungry and suffering shame.

The grown-ups have made this mess and they must be the ones to fix it. Make sure lunchtime shaming isn't being practiced at your kid's school. If it is, voice your concerns and opposition to the school administrators. Continue up the chain of command to the school board and lobby for other parents to take a stand against lunch shaming as well.

Check out any legislative efforts focused on reducing food insecurity and ending lunch shaming practices. Sen. Tina Smith and Sen. Ilhan Omar introduced the No Shame at School Act to address the overall problem of kids not being able to afford school lunch on a federal level. The act proposes a ban on shaming practices like the school publishing a list of students owing lunch money or stamping a child's hand. It also addresses the underlying issue of food insecurity by increasing the number of eligible children certified for free or reduced-price school lunches.

Kids who are living in some level of poverty are in desperate need of the village to step up. More than 20 percent of all children in the United States live in poverty. If you volunteer in your child's completely average classroom and read a book to five classmates, there's a good chance that one of those children lives in poverty.

Researchers argue that poverty is the single greatest threat to the well-being of children. It's a burden on their ability to concentrate and learn. It contributes to social, emotional, and behavioral problems. It hinders their mental and overall health. Millions and millions of children deal with this tremendous hardship during their developmental years.

There are some things you can do to help impoverished children in your village and combat the overall problem of children in poverty. Speak to employees at your child's school about what they're doing to help children in poverty. Some schools are great about having ways to help already in place—

sometimes you can give holiday gifts for children in need based on wish lists they've filled out. Sometimes they have food pantries you can donate nonperishable goods to so children in need can take them home to ensure they have something to eat. Sometimes you can donate extra school supplies. If your child's school doesn't have anything like this in place, bring up the idea and offer to help get it started.

As always, remind your kids to treat their classmates with universal kindness. You don't need to break down our country's economic state or talk about anything that makes any child different at all. But you, as the parent, should keep in mind that just as we grown-ups are facing invisible battles you may not know, these kids do as well. So it's important to speak to your kids about being kind and fair to everyone.

To address poverty on a larger scale, it's best solved with— *ding, ding, ding,* you guessed it—legislation. Politicians often spout out myths about families in poverty and paint an image of capable adults who choose not to work and live on government-provided resources instead, as if they're dining on lobster every night. But the Supplemental Nutrition Assistance Program (SNAP)—also known as food stamps—is extremely modest with an average benefit of $1.40 per meal. Even their guidelines call it a "bare-bones nutritionally adequate diet." More than half of parents with children in poverty *do* work, their jobs just aren't enough to lift them out of poverty. When politicians attack recipients of government assistance as "lazy," they're just perpetuating a myth and they're expecting you not to know any better. Also, when they advocate reducing funding for these benefits, making them more difficult to obtain while also easier to lose, or cutting them altogether, they're quite literally taking food from children in need.

Be mindful of what your representatives on the state and federal levels are proposing regarding these government assistance benefits. These benefits help families in poverty put food on the table, so taking them away could be devastating. Because so many children living in poverty have employed parents, advocate for higher wages as well. The federal minimum wage hasn't budged in more than a decade, and families feel the impact. Also, the vast majority of impoverished children are covered by public healthcare, and so we must protect coverage to keep families protected.

Even if voters and politicians insist on blaming impoverished adults for their circumstances (and it's so, so much more nuanced than that), the children living in poverty were simply born into it. If they could choose, I'm sure they would have a refrigerator full of food over bare pantries and getting their hands stamped "need lunch money" by the cafeteria employees. When legislators cut government benefits for the poor, they're hurting children. We need to do what we can to defend families in poverty. So, always keep these issues in mind, and make sure your representatives hear your thoughts. And maybe suggest Jeff Bezos downgrade one of his yachts instead of reducing a family's ration of beans. Just a thought!

You can make a difference in the lives of children outside of your own. At first, the task of being the village and keeping an eye on not only your children but children in your community can seem daunting. I can't even find two matching socks for my kid; how am I supposed to make a difference in the lives of children who aren't mine? Well, what's remarkable is that you can make a huge difference by doing small things.

Children and teens in the LGBTQ community experience a much higher rate of suicide than their heterosexual peers.

Lesbian, gay, and bisexual youth are nearly five times as likely to have attempted suicide compared to their heterosexual peers. For transgender youth, the numbers are even more disheartening. By the time transgender individuals reach adulthood, 40 percent of them have attempted suicide.

The underlying reasons that drive so many LGBTQ adolescents to depression and suicide are issues that affect them often more than their heterosexual peers—things like the rejection by their family, bullying, and physical or verbal harassment and abuse. Organizations such as The Trevor Project have a wealth of information and resources for LGBTQ youth, parents, educators, counselors, and virtually anyone who interacts with young people and wants to do their part in helping reduce these tragic statistics.

According to one study, transgender youths experience a drastic drop in their risk of depression and suicide when they're able to use their chosen name at work, school, with friends, and at home. How simple is that?! Transgender youth who could use their preferred name everywhere experienced a 65 percent decrease in suicidal attempts. It's a remarkably simple solution, and yet, it makes sense. If someone denied your identity and refused to call you by your name, it would probably be distressing to you, too. It takes very little effort to ask someone their name and preferred pronouns, and then use them correctly. But to be seen and recognized as your true and authentic self makes a huge difference.

I cannot even begin to list all the challenges and hardships children in your community potentially face. But the same strategy that makes such a tremendous difference in the lives of transgender youth can be applied to every child. They need to be seen for who they are, shown compassion, feel respected and worthy, and have their basic needs met.

There are children in need all around you. But by considering what their needs are and identifying the small ways you can help, you can make a huge difference.

Practice Community Care as You Practice Self-Care

We know self-care is a necessary part of feminism, activism, and a political act. But it's also—duh—completely focused on oneself. As discussed earlier, self-care is not just bubble baths and pedicures; it's work, and often really hard work. Sometimes, people cannot do that work themselves, and they need help from others just to survive.

Self-care is about nurturing and taking care of yourself, which sometimes includes engaging in therapy or taking the time to exercise. But to do those things, you have to have some degree of privilege. If you're struggling to find enough money to feed your family, you're probably not concerned about enjoying a lavish skincare routine. If you're too depressed to get out of bed, yoga probably isn't going to be enough to help. If you're struggling just to survive, you can't focus on trying to thrive.

That's when we need to have community care. We need to have people committed to being the village and stepping in to help people in need. We need to be fiercely compassionate and treat people with respect as we're empathetic to their needs.

You don't even have to go far beyond your village to practice community care. You probably already do this as you reach out to a friend who's been quiet or disconnected lately. You do it when you bring your beloved enchiladas to a grieving friend. When you do these small acts of kindnesses, you're recognizing that someone you care about may be having a difficult time caring for themselves. So, you're simply letting them know that you care and doing something to make caring for themselves a little bit easier.

Just like bringing a casserole to a friend, community care is about extending this courtesy outside your circle. It's about greeting people with kindness and empathy.

While self-care will help you as an individual and it likely will even help your family, it doesn't help big systemic issues. However, even taking small actions in community care does. Will standing beside a Black mother in a school board meeting in support of her son's natural hair do something to combat systemic racism? Yes! You could take out a decades-old racist dress code that does nothing but police natural Black hairstyles. Will making an effort to call a transgender teen by their chosen name make a difference in combating transphobia? Yes! You're setting an example to others by simply showing some basic decency and may even reduce the teen's risk of depression and suicide in the process.

You matter and you must take care of yourself, which is why self-care should be a mandatory part of your life. But just as you matter, so do all the people around you. Sometimes they need to hear that they matter, and they need a little help taking care of themselves. Self-care brings us closer to a more just and peaceful self. But community care brings us closer to a more just and peaceful world.

CHAPTER TEN

Check Your Privilege

"I am not free while any woman is unfree, even when her shackles are very different from my own."

-Audre Lorde

I n early 2017, my local Jewish Community Center received a bomb threat. Employees of the center and the local police force responded swiftly to evacuate and determined it was only an empty threat. This wasn't a surprise because over the previous two months, roughly one hundred Jewish organizations had received threats. It was just our turn.

It was alarming to have droves of children and adults evacuate a building where the Star of David flies on the flagpole and people gather to celebrate Jewish holidays and deepen their understanding of their Jewish heritage. But most of the people who go to the local JCC are taking cycling classes or doing community theater. Many of them aren't even Jewish, just like members of the local YMCA may not be Christian.

So as they were forced to evacuate their exercise classes and interrupt their swimming routines, it alerted many people to the growing issue of anti-Semitism the Jewish community faces. They had surely heard of the bomb threats all over the country previously. But now, they had to leave their workouts and rehearsals to consider that this wasn't just a threat to a building, it was a threat to a people.

For Jews, the alarm had been sounding for a while. The previous year, the presidential campaign was fueled by support from white nationalists, and a palpable division was establishing throughout our country. The ethos that the Holocaust began not with killing, but with words, was circulated as a grim warning. Most Jews have some level of vigilance no matter the political climate, but things felt different—more urgent, more defeating, scarier.

So although this was just a bomb threat in a widespread string of threats, and there was, just like the others, no bomb; action still needed to be taken. The threats were targeted to provoke fear and signal to Jews that our synagogues and community centers where we celebrate our Jewishness were not safe places. It was a message that we should be afraid. I was afraid, and I doubt I was alone in my fear. But no matter what terror existed, we did what Jews do and refused to be terrorized. A rally was organized at the Jewish Community Center to take a stand against anti-Semitism and show that we refused to live in fear.

Hundreds of people gathered to show support. Considering the Jewish community is pretty small and this crowd was even bigger than the Yom Kippur crowd, it was clear many of the people who showed up were allies. Under a large "We Stand Together" banner, I could see my rabbi, the district's Jewish congressman, and some other community leaders. Other than the occasional kippah in the crowd, I identified other groups who showed up to support the Jewish community.

I saw many church groups who wore T-shirts and signs letting everyone know their church stood with the Jewish community. A minister from one of the city's historically Black Baptist churches spoke. Muslim community members showed up just as Jewish community members show for them when they're the target of attacks, as they occasionally find themselves being. People held signs with the words "Prays well with others" and religious and spiritual symbols like the cross, Star of David, yin-yang, and the crescent moon and star below the words.

I'm ashamed to think about it now, but as I stood there, I thought about how alone I felt in a crowd of hundreds of people. My children were very young, and I didn't want to talk to a toddler whose world was still dinosaurs and Daniel Tiger about anti-Semitism yet, so I left them at home. I came alone. I looked at the churches that showed up and didn't see the names of churches where I knew people who attended. Instead of seeing who showed up, I was looking for people who didn't. I thought, *Why aren't they here? Don't they care? Don't they know what's happening?*

Then I watched as Sadiqa Reynolds took the stage. Reynolds represented the city's urban league which advocates for social and economic opportunities for African Americans and other under-served people in the community. She stood in front of the microphone beside other community leaders, looked over the crowd, and started sobbing.

Tears ran down her face and she said between the gasps what a beautiful thing it was to see the community stand together like this because she didn't see that very often. Much of the work Reynolds does is focused on the West End of the city, at least a fifteen-minute drive away from the JCC.

The West End is where Muhammad Ali grew up; all 1,100 square feet of his old house still stands in his memory. Through redlining, the systematic process of pushing minorities out of certain areas of town, many African Americans were forced to settle in the West End. Many families lived in the West End lived in extreme poverty, which is why some people like my very white, but very poor grandmother and her family lived there too. "Right down the street from Cassius Clay!" my Nanny would say.

Decades later, the area is still ravaged by extreme poverty fueled by a lack of jobs. It's a food desert without any grocery store full of fresh, healthy food. Despite a recent gentrification effort, housing is still quite cheap. (The local Black Lives Matter chapter purchased their first house for only five thousand dollars.) The West End is also the site of many gun violence incidents. In the past year, 75 percent of the city's homicides were in the area encompassing the West End.

The incidents of gun violence are unfathomable, but as the homicides continue to be reported on the news—sometimes as often as daily or more—people have become desensitized. It takes the incidents like that of the seven-year-old boy who was killed by a stray bullet as he sat at his kitchen table eating cake, to hold the public's attention for long. But, still, the crimes tend to go unsolved and the gun homicide rate tends to continue to increase. More lives—most of them Black—are senselessly lost.

There are community rallies of support for the Black community and victims of gun violence, sure. But I can't recall one where hundreds of allies and the congressman attended—one with the mayor making a statement condemning the violence. Usually, the Black lives lost are memorialized by a minute-long segment on the evening news and forgotten by the commercial break.

When incidents of police brutality occur and news stations share graphic videos of people of color being violently assaulted by the local police force, the most popular comments are ones justifying the use of force and saying things like: "That's what you get" and "Great job, officer." Showing support for the police and using the hashtag #BlueLivesMatter is a commonplace source of pride even though blue lives only exist in Smurfville, and officers choose to wear a uniform and have the choice to take it off. Meanwhile, Black Lives Matter activists advocate against the unjust killings of people who were senselessly killed due to the color of their skin and are labeled as extremists.

So, when an advocate for the Black community—one who has intimate knowledge of this hostile environment, sees the faces of extreme poverty, and comforts grieving family members who lost loved ones for no good reason—looks out into a huge crowd of allies, it's bittersweet because the Black community does not get the same support when they're in need.

I listened to Reynolds sob and noticed my rabbi place his hand on her shoulder, comforting her and hanging his head. She pleaded between sobs, "Please don't just rally today. We need you every day." It wasn't until this moment that I realized how misguided and self-interested I had been. When my community was threatened, hundreds of people supported me. I didn't know them, but they didn't have to know me to show up, and instead of recognizing this, I searched for the ones who didn't show up. Other groups are threatened every day, and no one shows up because we are so desensitized to their suffering.

This is how privilege manifests itself. I have privilege, but that doesn't mean I was immune to hurt at that moment. But because I didn't recognize my privilege at that moment either, I also completely denied the experience of someone with less privilege whose community is suffering more. I was so concerned about who was showing compassion to me, I didn't even notice someone needed that compassion too.

It's embarrassing to think about. It's hard to talk about a time when I was so self-interested, I didn't see someone else was hurting until I noticed the tears running down their cheeks. But recognizing these mistakes and weak moments is how I can learn to do better. I'll never be perfect; I'll continue to make mistakes. But recognizing these mistakes, talking about privilege, and practicing anti-racism in ourselves is the only way forward.

Recognizing Privilege

The first time a name was given to the invisible force of white privilege that is a rarely recognized, but omnipresent part of our lives was in an academic article by feminist scholar and anti-racism pioneer Peggy McIntosh who understood unpacking white privilege was integral to the study of women's issues and pursuing equality.

In her analytic essay, "White Privilege: Unpacking the Invisible Knapsack," Peggy McIntosh uses a brilliant metaphor to describe the privilege white people experience. As if the first name Peggy wasn't enough of a giveaway, McIntosh is a white woman who understands white privilege because she lives it. Her metaphor for white privilege was that white people are given an invisible knapsack full of "special provisions, assurances, tools, maps, guides, codebooks, passports, visas, clothes, compass, emergency gear, and blank checks." It is a *very* big knapsack.

In a deeply introspective process, McIntosh examined her privilege and listed experiences she could count on having virtually any time that her African American peers could not. Although she was breaking new ground on recognizing these disparities because the status quo for white people was to simply take these things for granted, the issues she listed more than thirty years ago are still extremely relevant today. Here are a few:

+ "I can if I wish arrange to be in the company of people of my race most of the time."

+ "I can go shopping alone most of the time, pretty well assured that I will not be followed or harassed."

+ "I can choose blemish cover or bandages in 'flesh' color and have them more or less match my skin."

+ "I can do well in a challenging situation without being called a credit to my race."

+ "I can be pretty sure that if I ask to talk to 'the person in charge,' I will be facing a person of my race."

+ "If I want to, I can be pretty sure of finding a publisher for this piece on white privilege."

—Peggy McIntosh, *White Privilege: Unpacking the Invisible Knapsack*

Bigotry and lack of representation are themes still relevant today. When I read McIntosh's list of examples, I think about how the same themes manifest in my life. I haven't been pulled over while driving in more than a decade. I can always find dolls that look like my kids. When I shop at Aldi and TJ Maxx, people assume I'm thrifty, not poor. I never have any trouble finding makeup in my skin tone. I've never experienced discrimination due to the color of my skin.

These examples of representation may seem very minor, especially if you are white and tend to take them for granted. But these small examples are just indications of living in a world where the default is whiteness. If you're white, think about the entertainment you like. Do you reminisce about *Friends* or *Girlfriends*? If you're in a doctor's office waiting room, do you pick up a copy of *People* or *Essence*? Which is your favorite show—*Modern Family* or *Black-ish*?

It's ok if you probably cried when Netflix took *Friends* out of their lineup, pick up *People* at the market, and not only watch *Modern Family*, but also follow all the cast members on Instagram and at the same time have never divulged in entertainment for Black audiences. If you're white, you're not the target demographic of magazines like *Essence*, but you are the target demographic for the other thirty women's magazines on the shelf.

Think about why you prefer entertainment with white actors in the starring roles and white celebrities on the magazine covers. A lot of white people start getting defensive and uncomfortable at this point in conversations about race. If you are already uncomfortable, work through that. You are not under attack.

You probably prefer media with white people if you're white. It's not groundbreaking. It just makes sense. If you're watching a TV show with people who look like you, you'll probably find it more relatable and possibly enjoy it more than a show with no one that looks like you. If you prefer media that features white people, that does not mean you are racist or is any indication of your feelings about minorities. It's just about representation. You're attracted to seeing people who look like you represented. It's natural.

Having white privilege in representation is being able to look at the entertainment and retail industries and seeing your race reflected. When you're white, the prime-time sitcoms usually feature people who look like you, and you can pick pretty much any bottle in the shampoo aisle assuming it's fine for your hair. Minorities are marginally represented, and more white people are always represented in entertainment, product advertisements, etc.

If you're white, even though your race tends to be the default, you've still probably felt unrepresented in some areas and have also experienced what it's like to be represented in some way when you weren't before. The average American woman wears a size somewhere between fourteen and eighteen, but the average model wears a size between two and four. It's frustrating to feel unrepresented, and it makes it difficult to shop online for clothing when the model doesn't look like you. But have you ever shopped online and saw a model wearing the outfit you want with a body type that resembles your own? It's liberating, helpful, and gives you a little extra confidence boost when you rock that outfit because representation matters.

Representation and privilege are not just black and white. White privilege is the most dominant and, due to its prevalence and unfairness, it deserves the majority of the conversation. But privilege is a spectrum encompassing many factors that contribute to someone's privilege.

If you follow McIntosh's knapsack metaphor (and I will because it's a great one), privilege awards you many more tools in your knapsack. Some people have an easy path full of opportunities to make their dreams come true because their knapsack is heavy, stuffed to the brim with tools to help them along the way. These people with the heaviest knapsacks full of the most privilege are probably white and probably male, so they experience very little, if any, discrimination. They worked hard in school, but it also helped that they were legacy applicants and their parents helped guide them to Ivy League schools. Their trust funds allowed them to begin their careers with a smooth transition. They may still struggle in some areas. They may work very hard. But the tools in their hefty Louis Vuitton knapsacks helped them navigate life much easier than if they didn't have as much privilege.

Then you have people with some medium-weight knapsacks they picked up at TJ Maxx. Maybe they come from a blue-collar, middle-class background. They're white, but also women so they do experience some natural injustice and face issues like such as pay disparity. Through their own merit, they were able to attend college as first-generation students but didn't know how to pay for it, so now they're deep in student loan debt. Their discounted knapsacks have some handy tools that have certainly helped them along the way, but they also have struggled and may continue to do so.

"Wow! You all have knapsacks?!" the people with little privilege ask in wonder. They don't have knapsacks; they carry around an old plastic grocery bag since their last trip to the corner store where they stretched their food stamps to buy enough beans to get through the week. Their sacks aren't empty, but they're very light. Depending on perspective, they may have privilege based on the fact that they were born in the United States and not in a war-torn, underdeveloped country. But they have very little inherent privilege that has helped them navigate opportunities in their lives because few opportunities ever presented themselves. They can't thrive because they're too focused on merely surviving.

Privilege is not merely about race, but it's mainly about race because we live in a country that has benefited from the oppression of racial minorities, specifically Native Americans and African Americans. If you're white, it doesn't mean your life has been without struggle. It simply means that being born white has not been part of an inherent struggle for you.

When you read the examples of people who carry heavy knapsacks full of privilege and one that are lighter, keep in mind the spectrum of privilege and how privileged you may be. If you were born wealthy, had parents who attended college, are white, healthy, insured, having savings in the bank, or educated—all of these factors contribute privilege. If you are an underrepresented minority, live in poverty, were born into poverty, do not have a college degree, or are disabled, those factors contribute to adversity you'll need to overcome to achieve what you want.

It's necessary to access and understand your own privilege and how that plays into your life compared to others with less privilege. When privileged people don't recognize their privilege, they tend to promote the old "pull yourself up by the bootstraps" philosophy to oppressed populations. But just like we're carrying knapsacks of different weights, it's unhelpful for someone of privilege to tell someone who isn't to pull themselves up by the bootstraps without taking the time to notice they didn't have any bootstraps.

Practice Anti-Racism

"We know how to be racist. We know how to pretend to be not racist. Now let's know how to be antiracist."

-Ibram X. Kendi

As a brilliant historian and author, Ibram Kendi declared in his guide to racial ethics *How to Be an Antiracist*, that there are only two schools of thought regarding racism—there is racism and there is anti-racism. Racists do not take a stand in opposing racist ideas and allow the racist ideas to flourish without taking a stand against them. Anti-racists understand that every racial group is equal, and there are no inherent rights or wrongs associated with any racial group, but anti-racists take it a step further and call out and destroy racist ideas when they are exposed, and that is what we need to do.

Even the most deplorable bigots understand that racism is cruelty that has contributed to horrors such as the senseless murders of Black people and genocides like the Holocaust. As such, even people who have been rightfully labeled as racists for espousing racist ideas refuse to accept that they are racists. David Duke is a neo-Nazi and former Grand Wizard of the Ku Klux Klan and was described by the Anti-Defamation League as perhaps America's most well-known racist and anti-Semite. In the new generation of neo-Nazi, there's white supremacist Richard Spencer, who coined the term "alt-right" and is such a shitty person he can't even complete a minute-long interview without a bystander punching him in the face.

But even the most notorious racists promoting racism today— Duke and Spencer—will not accept the term racist to describe themselves. Instead, they will deflect and claim to call someone racist is the real slur (and they call *us* snowflakes…) or they use the term racist to describe progressives who seek to defeat racism in one form or another. It's nonsensical, but even Nazis realize they have a PR problem.

So, no one wants to admit they're racist and no one wants to recognize any degree of racism in themselves. Everyone recognizes there is ugliness in racism, and they don't want to admit they have such ugliness within too. It's really hard work to look so deeply within yourself that you may see you exhibit signs of something you hate.

White people have become so uncomfortable with the issue of racism; we've chosen to separate ourselves from it. For one, we have the privilege and ability to do this. We don't directly face discrimination due to the color of our skin, so we can easily step away and say it's not our problem. We often proclaim that we're "colorblind," that we believe so deeply in racial equality we supposedly don't even notice physical differences in race. Because we did not individually steal humans from Africa and transport them through the Middle Passage to be our slaves or we don't don white hoods while shouting horrible, racist ideas, we insist we are not racist.

But racism isn't always that overt. To ignore the plight of racism is not compassionate, it's cruel. It allows racism like a plague to spread and gain power throughout our country before we admit that we're sick. Unless we're actually blind, we see color, and to say we don't just denies the experience of racism people of color face. It's factually unfair to ignore racism because it doesn't directly affect us as white people who don't experience discrimination. After all, we built systemic racism. We have benefited from the racist system whether or not it was our intent. It's not just callous to dismiss racism as not our problem, it's disingenuous because we made the problem.

It's not enough to do our best not to be racist. Not being a neo-Nazi with a platform is not commendable; that's a bare minimum standard of being a decent person. When we know that racism exists, but don't see ourselves as any part of the problem, we're taking a neutral position, and neutrality is always toxic to social justice.

As Holocaust survivor and prolific author Elie Wiesel wrote in The Night Trilogy (*Night, Dawn,* and *The Accident*) "We must take sides. Neutrality helps the oppressor, never the victim. Silence encourages the tormentor, never the tormented. Sometimes we must interfere. When human lives are endangered, when human dignity is in jeopardy, national borders and sensitivities become irrelevant. Wherever men and women are persecuted because of their race, religion, or political views, that place must—at that moment—become the center of the universe."

It's challenging to put any idea or action into a racist or anti-racist box, but it's a great exercise to change the way you think about racism and ensure you're doing your best to combat racism. Remember, "not racist" is not an option. That's a neutral position, and neutrality is fuel for racism. So if it's neutral—neither what you would find racist or anti-racist—then it's racist. *Ugh!* I know. Total downer. But not nearly as much of a downer as it is to know we live in a society that literally and figuratively beats Black people down while we allow it to happen. So, that's why we do this.

Let's take a look at some ideas and statements and determine if they're racist or anti-racist. As a reminder, if the idea in any way suggests that one racial group is inferior or superior to another racial group, it's racist. If the idea suggests racial groups are completely equal in all their apparent differences and that there is nothing right or wrong with any racial group, it's anti-racist. Those are your only choices and there are no levels. So, don't think *Eh, it's a little racist*. There are only two boxes—racist and anti-racist. Put these statements, ideas, and situations in one:

+ Laughing at a joke that promotes stereotypes and puts Black people in the punchline.

+ Telling a Black student they're "so articulate!"

+ Dismissing claims of racism as fancies of a society that has become too politically correct.

+ Locking car doors when a person of color walks by.

+ Flying the Confederate flag.

+ Explaining that being a woman who experiences gender oppression is just like experiencing racial oppression, so we're one and the same.

Ok. So, what do your boxes look like? Hopefully, your anti-racist box is still empty because none of those situations or statements did a damn thing to combat racism or could be labeled anti-racist. But, because anti-racism is the process of identifying and destroying racism, we've already completed the first step, and now let's see if we can transpose these racist statements to anti-racist ones.

+ Refuse to tolerate racist jokes. Jokes involving a racial or ethnic group aren't all inherently harmful, but it doesn't take an anthropologist to determine which jokes are racist and which ones aren't. Don't laugh. Don't smile. Don't attempt to be polite. Ask the jokester to explain the joke as if you don't understand and they're forced to dissect the racist tropes and expose themselves as a racist with bad jokes. Let them know their jokes suck and you don't want to hear them anymore.

+ Work on your perceptions of marginalized groups and the stereotypes that still exist in your head. This kind of statement implies an element of surprise because a minority is well-spoken that suggests you think most minorities are not articulate. Question if you exclaim things like, "You're so articulate!" only to marginalized people. Work on these issues internally. If you're impressed with someone, specifically tell them why. Admire their talent and discuss their most thought-provoking points.

+ Accept that you are always learning. If someone tells you said or did something offensive to a minority group, the correct response is "I'm sorry." Your ego is not more important than someone's hurt. Empathize and critically examine what you did or said. Atone by pledging to learn from the mistake and do better.

+ Actions like locking doors or grasping a purse when you're near a Black person imply that you associate crime or danger with Black people. That's racist, but the actions are familiar for a lot of people to the point that they're willing to dismiss the underlying racism. Reject this routine. If you feel the urge to do this, confront your racism at that moment, and remind yourself that this is racist behavior based on stereotypes and fearmongering.

+ Symbols like the Confederate flag have oppressive histories, which is why white supremacist groups tend to cling to them. Listen to people who are hurt by the image of the flag and do your research on the history if you're unclear about why it's associated with racism. If someone

insists on flying a flag to remember the Confederacy's
Civil War defeat, try flying a white flag instead!

✦	Never equate your experience living as a woman as equal
to any other group's experience with oppression. You
only know your personal experience. So if, as a woman,
you want to speak to the injustices women experience,
you certainly can and should do that, including speaking
about how those injustices affect your life and how they
make you feel. But, unless you are a member of another
marginalized group, you can never speak in the same
way about their experiences. It is not your story to tell.
If you're white, always keep in mind the white privilege
you were born with and practice anti-racism.

I use the word "practice" along with anti-racism, and I hope
you keep that term in mind. Anti-racism does not demand
perfection. It's quite the opposite, as you're embarking on an
introspective process and examining your personal biases and
racist tendencies. It's not something you can simply commit
to and accept that by rejecting racism, you are done. You
are never done. You must always understand you're looking
through the lens of your privilege.

Keep in mind that neutrality aids the oppressor, not the
oppressed. Examine everything related to race in the racist or
anti-racist dichotomy. When you're forced to make a choice
and determine whether something is one or the other, you
gain clarity about an action's accurate effect. Even if your
intentions were good and not overtly racist, if it doesn't
contribute directly to anti-racism, it does promote the notion
that one racial group is inferior to the other, and ultimately, it
hurts people.

It can be difficult to talk about racism. But avoiding these
discussions has minimized the struggles of the oppressed and

allowed racism to thrive. Overcome your discomfort and speak openly about how you practice anti-racism. This may be a new concept for others to consider and adopt themselves. We may not ultimately change the hearts and minds of people like David Duke and Richard Spencer. But by humbly examining ourselves and embarking on the journey of self-awareness and anti-racism practice, we can change our hearts and minds, and that can make all the difference.

CHAPTER ELEVEN

Raise Up Your Sisters

"Be the woman who fixes another queen's crown without telling the world that it was crooked."

−Anonymous

B e thin! (But not too thin.) Focus everything that you are into your role as a mother! (But if you want a career, you better work like you don't have kids.) Don't show signs of aging! (But, ack—don't wear too much makeup or admit you got Botox.) Be sexy! (But, not too sexy. Jeez, you're a mother!) Be feminine! (But not too feminine because femininity is inferior to masculinity.) Drink more water! Get enough sleep! Take your vitamins! (But not anti-depressants; try these essential oils and a hike instead.)

The pressure women and mothers face in our daily lives is maddening. We're expected to be everything to everyone—our children, our partners, our employers, society—to the point that we're held to an impossible standard. We cannot be all the things to all the people. We cannot sacrifice all our time and all of our energy without also sacrificing ourselves. It's not possible to devote our entire lives to how we can be of service to others and at the same time be true to ourselves and what fulfills us.

Much of the pressure and criticism mothers carry are an exclusively female experience and a consequence of living in a patriarchal society. So much of our behavior is harmful to women and treats them unfairly, which just deepens the inequality between the sexes. But what is maddening is that it's not just men dipping their toes in the misogynistic waters due to their self-interest. It's often women who push other women down and contribute to their oppression.

Millions of women chose to vote for a sexual predator who didn't have any foreign policy experience—beyond playing Battleship once—for president over the first woman candidate of a major party who had more experience than any male candidate before her. Women buy tabloids that mock women's bodies and feature zoomed-in images of cellulite. Few men have strong opinions about childbirth choices and infant feeding, but so many women are so passionate about the decisions other mothers make the conflict has been called the "Mommy Wars," as if we're all foot soldiers in a war even more pointless than the ones our country engages in.

All of these things strengthen a patriarchal system that just brings women down. Some women can be so uncomfortable about women's issues and the pursuit of equality, they reject the feminist label. It tends to have a negative connotation based on myths and misconceptions. Feminism is considered radical. Radical! Feminism is simply advocacy based on the belief that men and women are fundamentally equal. The rejection of this notion in 2020 is radical.

Since people are resistant to the feminist label, they're not keen on being labeled misogynists either. But misogynists exist.

Would you consider the United States a place where men hold primary power and dominate areas of political leadership, social privilege, moral authority, and overall control?

Well, let's think. On the political leadership front, we've had forty-five male presidents, zero women, and men still make up the majority of Congress. So, check there. Regarding social privilege, men have more unearned privilege than women, and men have more authority over women in the workforce and gender roles at home. Check. From Moses to Socrates to Marx, whatever religious or philosophical influences helped shape your worldview, it was probably a dude, and men remain to dominate figures in moral authority. Check. Who holds the most control in the decisions that affect your life? Men possess the most power and women can't even get a pap smear at Planned Parenthood without finding herself in an evergreen controversy about who her body belongs to. So, check, check, check. We live in a patriarchy.

More women are living in the United States than men. We have the numbers. Why do we still live in a patriarchal society? Well, because we allow it.

We can't point fingers and blame men for the issues women face and ignore our complicity. Women throughout history have contributed to the oppression of women and stood against their liberation. Maybe we would have equal protection for women in a constitutional amendment if not for Phyllis Schlafly. It was the founding fathers that omitted our existence from the constitution, but it was our fellow women that kept us out. Maybe we didn't create the patriarchal structures that oppress us, but we've largely tolerated their existence and many of us continue to do so.

We can't be feminists who work to combat misogyny without looking within ourselves. We can't demand better treatment when we treat each other so terribly. If people are hesitant to embrace the feminist label, they sure as hell don't want to be labeled misogynists. But how can we have a patriarchal society where misogynistic ideas reign without any misogynists? We have to recognize our own internalized misogyny and practice anti-misogyny.

Just like the dichotomy of racism and anti-racism, imagine there is only misogyny and anti-misogyny. Your statements and actions regarding gender have to be put in one of those two boxes. Misogyny is the contempt for or ingrained prejudice against women and it exists in our lives and society in a myriad of ways. You may not even recognize it as misogyny when it happens because you're so used to its existence. Anti-misogyny is just feminism—the advocacy of equality between the sexes and belief that's they're fundamentally equal.

When you're presented with an idea or statement regarding women, think about if it promotes feminism and raises women up or if it furthers misogyny and brings women down. No middle ground; don't overthink it. Just consider if a situation or statement made concerning gender helps promote equality between the sexes or contributes to our inequality and oppression. If it has to be one or the other, which one would it be? Just like the anti-racism exercise earlier, take a look at these statements and think about if they would be an example of misogyny or feminism.

✦ Saying, "I'm not like the other girls" or "I just don't get along with other women."

✦ Being relentlessly asked when you'll be having kids,
    more kids, or stop having kids by someone other than
    your partner.

✦ A coworker telling a sexist joke.

✦ Being dismissed as moody because "it must be that time
    of the month."

✦ Not believing a woman could be president.

If you had to pick misogyny or feminism, they would be
misogynistic, right? Right. None of these micro misogynistic
moments help champion the cause of women's equality. So,
let's break down why these statements are problematic and
how you can reframe the argument leaving out the misogyny.

✦ If someone says you or they are "not like the other girls."
    You would first think, *what the hell is wrong with the
    other girls?* It's meant as a compliment as if most women
    stereotypically have unbecoming personality traits. But
    not you or them! You don't act like those other awful
    women. You're different. You're a cool girl. Maybe you
    like a cold beer while you watch football with the guys.
    (Go sports!) However you choose to vaguely step outside
    your stereotypical gender role, you're praised for it. The
    problem behind the praise is that it implies if you're "not
    like the other girls" and that's positive, the vast majority
    of other women are flawed. That's just foolish and a
    misogynistic way of thinking because it belittles women
    and pits them against each other.

✦ Nosy Nellies getting all up in your uterus and asking
    when you're going to start having kids or have more
    kids or stop having kids are another example of a
    well-meaning, but misogynistic practice. Men are not
    typically asked nearly as much as their female partners
    about their family planning status. But women are asked

the status of their uteruses approximately every six hours of their childbearing years. It suggests a woman's evergreen goal should be tied to mothering, and well, maybe it isn't. Maybe she's been struggling to get pregnant. Maybe she's suffered multiple losses. Maybe she doesn't want children. Maybe she doesn't want any more children. Maybe it's none of your damn business, Karen. Stop.

✦ If someone tells a sexist joke in the workplace, it's a total jerk move. The woman coworker is held hostage listening to the lame joke because she's at *work* and sometimes the coworker having a good, knee-slapping laugh at the expense of women is also the woman's superior. So she is faced with the awkward choice of speaking up or trying to be polite so she doesn't appear to lack a sense of humor. Sexism and sexual harassment have become common workplace dilemmas women have learned to navigate in a way that doesn't kill their careers. But any tolerance of sexism allows it to continue. If someone tells you a sexist or sexual joke that makes you uncomfortable, call them out. You could pretend you don't understand and let them explain the punchline until they realize they're being a sexist jerk or you can tell a witty, sexist joke with men in the punchline in a deadpan tone so they understand how ridiculous they sound.

✦ Any comments about it being "that time of the month" whenever a woman shows any iota of emotion is an unfair cheap shot. It's misogynistic in that dismisses women's real feelings as a mere biological side effect of something they don't understand. It's meant to shame the woman and offer an excuse for her expressing herself in a way that isn't completely calm, permissive, and rosy. If someone dismisses you in this way or talks about your monthly cycle as if it's a regular phenomenon that regularly turns you into a monster among us, either let them know it's super inappropriate to talk about a woman in that manner. Or double down and take the opportunity to discuss modern menstrual cups and the ins and outs of periods since they're so comfortable discussing it.

✦   Disqualifying major political party candidates based on their sex is an egregious sin that so many people are sadly guilty of committing, and it results in women being woefully underrepresented in political office. Men and women are inherently equal. There's nothing about a man that makes him better suited for a political office. If you as a voter consider a candidate the most qualified and preferable above the others and he happens to be a man, that's fine. You *should* vote your conscience and choose the candidate you believe is best for the job. I'm not asking anyone to pander or always vote for a woman no matter what.

I'm just asking to give women candidates a fair shot. They are not getting that right now. Everything from their salaries to their parenting to what they wear is scrutinized more than any policy position a man holds. They have to constantly fight for media attention to prove that they're worthy of standing on a debate stage with a man. They inevitably outwork their male peers, perfect their platforms, and pad their resumes to the point that a man with the same experience would look flawless.

But they fall short because too many voters take one look at them and say, "Meh. I just don't think a woman can do it."

Ugh. If we're ever going to shatter that Oval Office's glass ceiling, we have to kill this bullshit argument. Oh boo, you think women are too emotional to be president so you're going to vote for the guy who flirts with waging World War III on

Twitter between Fox News commercial breaks? It's offensive to the woman candidate who never gets the same shot other candidates do simply based on her sex. But it's also offensive to all women.

Think about what kind of message this rhetoric sends to our daughters about what they *can't* do. If an unqualified reality TV show host can be president of the United States, anyone can be president. (Maybe we took the "anyone can be president" adage too far, actually...) I refuse to live in a world that denies our brilliant daughters the dream of achieving our nation's highest office when that keeps them dreaming and gives them hope.

Stop counting out women candidates as if you're doing them a favor. Be fair and objective when you're making your choices, and don't hold women to an exclusive, impossible standard. When you overhear other people dismissing women candidates simply because they're women (even if they do it under the guise of "Well, I just don't know if *other* people will vote for a woman"), call it out as bullshit.

These micro misogynistic moments are such a frequent, universal occurrence, we often excuse them as harmless. But they aren't. They contribute to the patriarchy we live in and the oppressive policies that hold us down. They influence women to look at other women as their natural adversaries. They keep women out of the White House.

We have to practice feminism as the antithesis of misogyny much like we practice anti-racism. We have to be ruthlessly self-aware and examine our statements and actions for misogyny. We have to practice and mindfully behave in a feminist way because we will screw up. No need to wallow on our missteps, just learn and move forward.

Consciously consider how your statements and actions contribute to misogyny, and take a vow to change so we can burn the patriarchy to the ground.

Declare a Ceasefire on the Mommy Wars

Suit up, troop. Get your yoga pants on. Put your hair into a messy bun atop your head. Pack a baggie full of Cheerios. Meet your battle buddies at the park. You've been deployed to...the Mommy Wars.

The Mommy Wars are fought between fellow moms who have divided themselves into various parenting positions. Pro-vaccination vs. anti-vaccination, unmedicated childbirth vs. give-me-all-the-drugs during labor, exclusive breastfeeding vs. fed is best, working moms vs. stay-at-home moms, it goes on and on. The battlegrounds are found in mom's online groups, playgroups, kids' schools, and your own head. You don't even get a notice to report to duty before you find yourself amidst a battle.

No matter how sure you are of the choices you make as a parent, it feels deeply uncomfortable to have someone let you know they were the wrong ones because all you want is what's best for your kid. But no matter what decision you make, someone out there thinks it's the wrong one, and they might be anxious to tell you about it. The sanctimonious moms—or sanctimommies for short—are ready and waiting to let you know what your kid will be divulging to their therapist in twenty years.

When you first become a parent, just grasping the fact that you are now responsible for a little life is absolutely mind-blowing. Sometimes I make slice-and-bake cookies and have to dig the wrapper out of the trash because I forgot the instructions. I've never changed a furnace filter. I often don't notice I'm still wearing slippers until I'm dropping my kid off in her preschool classroom. So—me—a parent. What a concept.

But when you become a parent, there are also countless decisions to be made that only you can make. When you're new to a task—like parenting—it can be overwhelming and easy to second-guess yourself. All you want is what's best for your child. So, you fear not making the best decision. This task of endless decision-making paired with the novelty of having a new child is the perfect recipe for insecurity. Add in your standard challenges of being a parent, throw in a dash of stress at home, and maybe a dash of postpartum anxiety, and you're lucky most of us boil some water for boxed mac and cheese.

So when another mom inquires about your decisions and then immediately tells you you're wrong, it's a blow. It hurts. It worries you. You think *Oh, shit. Is there aluminum in vaccines and is that bad? Oh, I thought this school was ok, but apparently, it's trash and we need to move. Oh, I got an epidural because I felt like a honey badger was ripping through my uterus, but I guess I should have powered through.*

Much of the advice given by foot soldiers in the Mommy Wars aren't exactly something worth publishing in *The Lancet*. It's often driven by sanctimommies with Google university degrees, fearmongering, and occasionally a bit of truth. When everything is new and you're so committed to giving your new child every possible advantage by making the right decisions, it's easy to be so blinded by bad advice that you do silly things.

When I was a new mom, I did so many things that, in hindsight, sound absolutely insane. But at the time, I was so heavily influenced by fellow moms who sounded extremely sure of themselves, they seemed like very reasonable decisions. I was struggling to get pregnant and I heard a vaginal steam might help so I...*sigh*...steamed my vagina. When I got pregnant, I shopped for blankets to place over my belly to neutralize electromagnetic waves and protect my little bean from radiation caused by everyday devices. When I was in labor, I waited through a full twenty-four hours of active labor—while also receiving the max dose of Pitocin—before getting an epidural because I was so convinced I needed to go unmedicated.

Now I cannot believe that was ever me. *I* actually went shopping at my local health food store to brew a lovely tea...for my vagina. *I* actually was going to buy a magic blanket so my fetus wouldn't be harmed from the laptop radiation as I read more pseudoscience blog posts. *I* never got a medal for going twenty-four hours without an epidural, and once I finally got that sweet epidural nectar, my labor finally started progressing.

Mommy War soldiers smugly say, "Know better, do better!" when they disapprove of a stance another mom makes. The gist is that once you learn more information about a topic, you're better equipped to make the best decision. The gist is solid. But the concept has been completely mutated and equates knowing to saying because there's not always any truth to what they "know."

Mommy bloggers who dabble in pseudoscience and mom-shaming are three-star generals in the Mommy Wars. They don't just insist some decisions are best, they belittle mothers who make different decisions as if they just don't care about their children. They back up their claims with thinly veiled pseudoscience. They're almost always selling you something to cure all of what ails you. "Your kid doesn't need all those chemicals; they just need lavender essential oils! And I just happen to sell them!" they say. It's deceptive; it's fallacious; it's just mean.

The evidence to support one decision or another is often scarce or nonexistent. The difference between breastfeeding and bottle feeding (a hot Mommy Wars topic!), for example, is negligible. Infant formula has come a long way and is a blessing for so many families. Sometimes the supposed benefits of breastfeeding are things like claiming breastmilk is free. Well, it's only free if you consider women's time meaningless. It's a lot of work, and it's just not for every woman. Common issues such as medications, post-traumatic stress from sexual assault, feeding issues, and cancer are all barriers to breastfeeding. To make blanket statements that breastfeeding is best for every family is unfair and untrue. Fed is best. In a few years, they'll all be going to be eating granola they found under the couch, anyway.

The real problem is that no matter how silly these arguments sound, they can be harmful. If a mother is struggling with her mental health and her antidepressant is not compatible with breastfeeding, that mother does not need shame—she needs a can of formula. Moms have it hard enough; no one needs a fellow mom to make things more difficult.

Much of these decisions involve the suffering of women. I've heard so much anecdotal evidence about how unmedicated childbirth is best with quips like, "Don't you want to fully experience giving birth?" I don't know; would you want to fully experience a root canal? Coping with indescribable pain is not necessarily every mother's ideal memory of their childbirth experience.

Insecurity is the underlying cause fueling the Mommy War flames. I'm one of those people who can't even decide where we're going to dinner. It's natural to feel insecure about a decision with other possibilities. It can also be difficult to make an unpopular decision. Some people overcompensate for this insecurity by proudly proclaiming it was the correct decision and everyone else is wrong. Then, boom. Everyone's hammering away at their keyboards and getting snippy with each other at playgroup.

Now I know better, and I do better. I could not muster up a single crap about what another mom thinks about my parenting decisions. My kids are loved, cared for, and safe. I have liberated myself from the pressures and disapproval from other moms.

I've devised a pretty simple plan of action for when I assert my own opinion in the mundane parenting decisions of others—I don't. Unless a child is truly at risk of abuse and neglect, there's little point in intervening. If a choice interferes with the well-being of other children such as not vaccinating or a parent ignoring their little hellion while he goes apeshit in the mall play place, then I'll voice my concerns. If a mom friend specifically asks about a parenting decision, I'll share whatever would be helpful to her.

But as far as making the decisions, moms are the best ones to do that. I know that they're perfectly capable and loving, and I completely trust moms to make the best decisions for their families. Moms need support, not shame.

Show Some Love

Shortly after I became a new mother, I took my first trip out of
the house with a baby. We went to the post office, and I packed
enough things for a weekend. I had blankets, pacifiers, and an
extra set of clothes in my gigantic diaper bag. I finally exited
the car with my infant in a baby carrier resting on my chest
and the diaper bag on my shoulder as if the baby might need a
change during this two-minute-long errand, five minutes away
from home.

I watched in sleep-deprived wonder as a veteran mother loaded
at least three kids into the minivan parked next to my car. She
looked tired, too, but a very different kind of tired—fatigue that
appeared well-maintained. She wrangled them all into their
seats with the skill of an experienced choreographer. Once
she pressed the automatic doors, she turned and locked eyes
with me, a new dazed and confused mom with not enough
rest and too many pacifiers. She gave a friendly laugh and a
sincere smile.

She could have told me anything at that moment. She could
have told me I'll never sleep restfully again. She could have told
me about all the challenges I have ahead of me. She could have
told me puberty is hell. She could have told me to stop staring
like a weirdo. But instead, she held her hands out for emphasis
as she said, "You are going to have *so* much fun." Then she
smiled and drove away in her minivan, which looked like a
menagerie for children.

I was so lost, so tired, I don't think I even responded. I think
I just nodded as if to say, *Ok, promise?* But I've thought about
that little act of kindness and often it helped me push forward.

That short little message felt like an initiation into motherhood, and it helped me stay grounded.

Sometimes, I'd remember that moment and tell myself to just relax and have fun because the kids won't be little for long. When the exhaustion would start to catch up to me, I'd remind myself that this time is fleeting. When my toddler learned to unlock the bathroom door in less than thirty seconds, thus eliminating any privacy I had to even poop, I'd remind myself that the teenage years when they're too embarrassed to be hugged at school drop-off are coming. Just have fun. *I'm going to have so much fun*, I'd remind myself. And I have.

The kindness shown to me by that one mother has influenced the way I speak to other mothers. I never aim to be disingenuous about the real struggles of motherhood and am always willing to discuss my own experience with issues such as postpartum depression if it may help another mom. But I always try to stay positive with new moms. New moms get bombarded by horror stories about episiotomies and unsolicited advice about parenting choices. I think they just need someone to see them, smile, and say, "Hey. You're doing a great job. You're a wonderful mom. It's going to be ok."

When you see moms out, look for the ones who might need just a reassuring smile or a quick comment. If you see a mom holding a toddler with one arm because they're doing that thing when they turn into a sack of potatoes and just scream louder than you thought a child who can't even put on their own pants could possibly scream, don't judge. They already feel terrible. You can just smile and say, "We've all been there, mama." Those are the moments where parenting skills are really tested. So if you see a mom keep her cool while her kid is losing their shit, commend her by saying something like, "Hey, good job back there. I saw you kept calm, didn't back down, and I know that's not easy."

This courtesy shouldn't be limited to mothers. Celebrate the successes of other women. When your friends or acquaintances accomplish something great, congratulate them. Even if they're in the same field or maybe accomplishing something you desperately want to, don't allow your competitive nature or cynicism get in the way of celebrating someone who deserves celebration.

There seems to be pressure put on women not to announce or discuss their triumphs as not to appear too arrogant. The phrase "attention whore" is often used. That's trash. If you accomplished something, whether it's dropping your kid off at daycare for the first time without either one of you crying or getting a promotion at work, you deserve to celebrate! Share your success if you want to share it. Applaud yourself; you should be proud! Your story of how you got from point A to point B and accomplished something can be another woman's guide. Maybe someone with similar dreams can accomplish the same goal with your guidance and example.

One silly way I like to raise other women up is just verbalizing my internal monologue. I used to notice all the time I could admire another woman in my head and then those thoughts would just remain in my head. So I just started being more open with my thoughts. If I saw a woman with a fierce outfit and a stunning lip color, I used to think to myself, *Wow, she looks great. I like her style.* So, now if I have that thought, I just say to her either in person or on social media, "Wow! You look great. I like your style." Maybe she already knows and doesn't need the reassurance, but it's still a nice moment of appreciation and solidarity.

I don't keep compliments and nice thoughts in my head anymore. When someone has a talent or knack for something, I tell them how I admire that. When someone has a heart for giving, I tell them how much that's appreciated. I spent my time with close friends whom I love like family, and so I tell them out loud "I love you" when I see them. All these things are tiny gestures, but they've made a big impact in my own life as I'm more open and honest with the kindness I have in my heart for others, especially women.

Whatever your aspirations may be, I recommend you seek out women who have either accomplished what you seek to accomplish or are on the same path. Even if they're technically your competition, you may find you can achieve more when you support each other. I've found myself so humbled and amazed by the kindness of strangers who have helped me when I had little to offer them beyond my appreciation. As I sought to write my first book, I loved seeing other writers unbox their books and celebrate getting new deals and reviews. Even though I wasn't there yet, I felt myself become so inspired for others and sincerely excited for them.

The culture of misogyny—and internalized misogyny—has made the task of being a woman too often a hostile one. We have too many expectations, catcalls, societal pressure, and not enough kindness and clothing with pockets. Treat women you encounter not as your natural competition or adversaries, but rather as fellow sisters also just trying to navigate this wild world. Recognize other women's challenges and accomplishments, and be mindful of your behavior so you can do your part to raise other women up, not be someone else to bring them down.

PART IV

Taking a Stand

CHAPTER TWELVE

The Personal Is Still Political

"The personal is political" has been a feminist rallying cry older than most of our parents and is still true today. It's been impossible to separate being a woman with the role politics plays in our lives. Everything from our bodies to how we raise our children is politicized.

Occasionally, women will shy away from political and topical issues citing the ugliness and divisive nature of politics, saying, "I just don't get into politics." Some women have this choice to live as far removed from politics as they can be. But their lives can never be completely removed from politics.

A woman can say she doesn't like to be involved in politics. But the bank who manages her mortgage is involved in politics. Her representative who votes regarding the taxes she pays is. Her accessibility to healthcare is contingent on the political structure. The quality of her kid's school is affected by politics. Ignoring the role politics plays in our lives only makes an oppressor's role easier.

For those with less privilege, the stakes are much higher. Many people don't have the luxury of "not being into politics" because they are well aware of the oppressive role politics plays in their lives from the accessibility of affordable housing to healthcare to being subjected to discrimination and violence. Choosing not to engage in politics is not only self-destructive, it's cruel to those who don't have the choice.

After the election of 2016, many women had an epiphany as they saw how politics affects our country and their lives, no matter their political involvement. Many women could not stay silent any longer and took to the streets to voice their opposition even though they'd never been politically engaged before. This type of political engagement is overdue, necessary, and invigorating.

But just as many white women neglected politics until they witness a shift that was no longer possible to ignore, we cannot ignore any groups of women. For many marginalized communities and women of color, the 2016 election was not the same shock it was to many white women. It was years of heightened bigotry and pain coming to fruition.

It's a beautiful thing to have so many women finally engaged and concerned about what is happening in the United States and beyond. But we must not be concerned with only what affects us directly, we must always consider what the personal being political means for others.

What this looks like in activism is to be mindful of your focus. You've identified the issues that you are most passionate about and likely have your reasons why you're so impassioned. When you're advocating for change, be mindful of your perspective and privilege while looking at the full scope of the issue. For example, if gun violence is one of your key issues, don't focus solely on preventing school shootings because you can picture your child as a potential victim. Your concern is valid and school shootings are a horrific issue that should never exist, much less to the degree that they do in the United States.

However, if that's one of your key issues, you must also examine how the issue of gun violence affects others. If you want to combat gun violence, it's not enough to focus solely on school shootings. The odds of any child being killed in a school shooting are extremely low, about one in 614 million. However, gun violence is the first leading cause of death among Black children, who are often killed in their own homes. Seven-year-old Dequante Hobbs Jr., was killed in my community by a stray bullet as he sat eating a bedtime snack at his kitchen table.

I understand it's not simply about odds. Reducing gun violence is one of my priorities and key issues I care about. I was lobbying for an extreme risk protection order (or "red flag") bill along with Sandy Hook Promise founder Mark Barden. I wanted the honor of thanking Mark for all the work he's done and continues to do, including traveling to the Kentucky state capitol to spend just a couple of hours advocating for a gun reform law bill.

But, throughout the day, I kept putting off meeting him. For those who didn't know his story, Mark carried a photo of his son Daniel as he pleaded with lawmakers to act on combating gun violence. In the photo, you see a precious little boy with red hair that curls at the bottom and a toothless grin who is forever seven years old because he was viciously murdered at along with twenty-six others at Sandy Hook Elementary School.

When I finally mustered up enough courage to speak with Mark and shake his hand, he was so warm and kind. I told him that I also had a seven-year-old son—also named Daniel. When I told him this, I watched his eyes fill with tears and his face seemed to reflect the fear and sympathy I was feeling. I was avoiding him because I couldn't stand to look another parent in the eye who was living my worst nightmare. I had a hard time separating Mark's activism and grief from my thoughts of my seven-year-old Daniel and what kind of world he lives in.

Mark hugged me as I tried—unsuccessfully—not to sob on his shoulder. Then he looked me in the eye and asked, "Would you please give your Daniel a big hug…from me?"

After looking into the eyes of a parent whose child was that one in 614 million, I understand how meaningless of a statistic that can be. One is too many. We vowed as a country never again when the shooting happened at Sandy Hook in 2012. But since then, as of this writing, there have been 2,379 more mass shootings.

I understand how emotion can intertwine with political issues, and I don't even think that's necessarily bad. We shouldn't allow ourselves to look away or become desensitized to horrors happening. We should allow our emotions to motivate political action.

In the example of gun violence, just because school shootings are rare, that does not mean you can't advocate preventing future school shootings, motivated by your own love and fear for your children. Every school shooting is horrific. Every life lost is precious. Ending school shootings is a worthy cause and to be clear, I am not asking you to shift your focus away.

Instead, I'm asking you to keep the full scope of the problem in mind. Sticking with the example of combating gun violence, the common-sense measures you may advocate for are universal background checks, preventing domestic abusers from obtaining firearms, preventing someone in a mental health crisis from obtaining a firearm, increasing access to gun locks, reforming the police's use of force standard, etc.

When you look at the full scope of gun violence and the people affected, you're in a better position to combat the root issue. If you just focused on school security, that may prevent some school shootings, but it doesn't do anything to help people more likely to be killed by firearms. However, when you take a step back and approach the issue of gun violence with a big picture perspective, change can happen beyond your child's school. Those common-sense measures I mentioned combat the more common instances of gun violence including domestic violence, suicides, homicides, accidental deaths, and unjust police shootings, while also preventing school shootings.

The personal has been political, is still political, and will probably always be political. It's not only ok to allow your personal life to influence your political activism, it's a wonderful motivation to keep yourself driven and impassion others. But always be mindful of what the personal being political looks like for others.

Moms Are Natural Activists

When I've told people I'm writing a book about the intersection of motherhood and political activism, some people just looked at me as if I had an actual unicorn horn growing out of my forehead.

Political activism and motherhood should not be a foreign concept. Not every mother is at home knitting. Some of them are knitting pink pussy hats for the next Women's March. Some of them don't know how to knit and spend all their time mobilizing their community to enact social change. But activism is happening, and mothers are leading the charge.

When you look to the leaders of the resistance that has emerged in the last several years, you'll notice that many of the most influential are women. But many of them are also mothers. They may openly discuss the intersection of motherhood and political action such as Senator Elizabeth Warren, who describes herself as a mom to Amelia, Alex, Bailey, and the Consumer Financial Protection Bureau, or you just may not have realized that your favorite activists are also mothers like you.

One stay-at-home mom was folding the endless laundry produced by her family of five children when she heard the news that twenty children—no older than first grade—were killed in their elementary school. As she watched covered of the inconceivable tragedy, she sobbed. But as she listened to political pundits discuss the senseless murder of so many children as if it were an inevitable mishap, sending their thoughts and prayers, her heartache turned to anger. The next day, her anger morphed into action.

As a mom, she believed she could rally other moms to work together to combat gun violence. By the next day, she had created a Facebook page with seventy-five like-minded mom friends to support the cause. By the next year, the group had grown to 130,000 members and had chapters operating in every state. By 2017, the group had four million members, and that stay-at-home mom who was sobbing in front of a pile of laundry, Shannon Watts, was being called the NRA's worst nightmare.

Realizing the threat Shannon represented, the NRA attacked her directly and publicly for the first time with the headline "Not Watts She Seems" and focused their ridicule on her role as a stay-at-home mom with an illustration of

Shannon's head superimposed on a cartoon June Cleaver-
style dress surrounded by relics of their perceived notion
of motherhood—a feather duster, an iron, and a spatula, to
name a few.

This is still what so many associate with being a mother. Many
believe that to be a mother is to flip pancakes and dust the
furniture. Misogynists will lead you to believe that concepts
like politics and any type of political activism are beyond the
role of a mother. But they're wrong. This resistance is being
led by mothers like Shannon Watts who fold laundry and form
a grassroots movement powered by an army of fierce moms
just like her.

Shannon is an incredible activist, but beyond her passion and
drive, there's little that separates her from other moms. She
didn't have a following of thousands of people waiting to be
mobilized before she began Moms Demand Action. She didn't
have millions of dollars to pour into the group to get it started.
Her success has been due to her willingness to take a stand, her
refusal to back down, and her strength in finding her voice.

The resistance is led by moms. Not just any moms, but
moms much like yourself. Take a closer look at the activists
you admire and see yourself in them. You are capable of
turning your grief into anger and that anger into action,
just like Shannon. But perhaps the largest impact you can
make in the world is in the way you raise your children to
be compassionate, strong, fiery activists ready to change the
world, just like their mama.

Mom the Activist

Much like people may have misconceptions about motherhood being a natural pairing with political activism, many people also have misconceptions about what political activism looks like in practice. Some people picture political activists as hugely influential people with thousands of people supporting them and feminist tropes like burning bras in the street.

But activism is much simpler and more accessible than that. There is no minimum number of Twitter followers required. There are no annual dues. The time required can be managed while you're managing your role as a mother and only as demanding as you feel confident you can handle. You can engage in political activism and blend activism with your family-friendly lifestyle fairly seamlessly.

Activism is simply the effort to advocate for some type of social change. This typically manifests in the form of protests and big events such as the Women's March but can also take place in social media campaigns that don't even require you to leave your house or wear real pants. Anyone can and should be able to become an activist if they want to. It's important to keep activism accessible and freely available to all who want to engage.

So, what are some practical ways you could exercise activism?

You can vote. Foreign interference in our elections notwithstanding, we do live in a democracy, and we all have a voice. About 55 percent of eligible voters voted in the 2016 election. There are indeed many obstacles to voting that disenfranchise voters such as voter ID laws and inconvenient polling times. But most voters who didn't vote didn't cite these inconveniences as reasons they didn't report to the polls.

Instead, when asked why they skipped voting on election day, the majority shrugged and said they weren't interested.

Voting is one of the most accessible, simple ways you can participate in our democracy. So, the most important thing you need to do is ensure that you vote. Don't just vote in the presidential election every four years, vote in every election. Take a moment to research the candidates in your local and state elections. Talk to your local friends and family reminding them to vote.

The process of voting in the United States is not always easy. Elections are held on a weekday and the polls close at the same time many people get out of work. You must make sure you're registered. In many states, you must bring and show your ID. So, be mindful of these obstacles and identify people who do not vote as a result. Let them know about other options in your area such as early voting and absentee ballots. Make sure your voice and the voices of those around you are heard on election day.

Another way you can engage in political activism and not even leave your home is to write letters to the editor of your local newspaper. This is an old school method of activism that is sometimes shockingly effective. Some people still read newspapers; who knew? It's very easy—you just need to search for an email address to send a letter to the editor from your local newspaper. Take a moment to write a concise argument about your position and a summary of the issue of no more than about five hundred words. Send that baby and see what happens.

You can write letters to the editor about national issues such as your concern with bigotry and bullying language coming out of the White House, your endorsement of local candidates running for political office, or local issues affecting your community such as a proposed change to the school system.

Just a couple of years ago, I was horrified to learn that a convicted sex offender who had to plead guilty to three felony counts for child exploitation had been elected as deputy chief of my small town's fire department. The fire department routinely interacts with children in the community, including my kid's preschool which takes regular field trips to the firehouse.

As a taxpayer, I contributed to the salary of this sex offender. But I didn't get a vote; no one in the community did. Employees of the fire department conducted an internal election and refused to nominate anyone other than the sex offender who had been stripped of his certifications by the state. When confronted with these facts, employees of the fire department chose to defend the sex offender.

I was angry and felt I had little recourse. So I wrote a letter to the editor of my local newspaper explaining my frustration and suggested that the local firehouse elect someone else as deputy fire chief, perhaps someone else who did not have a prior conviction of terrible crimes against vulnerable children. Quite a few outraged citizens shared the letter and expressed their outrage. The fire department did not respond.

When I sent the letter to the newspaper, I also sent the same letter to each member of the board that oversaw funding for the fire department and gave the department $1.5 million that year. Later, that board voted unanimously to cease funding for the fire department and replace them with a new department without a convicted sex offender at the helm.

I cannot tell you my one little letter to the editor contributed to this change. I can only say that in this instance, I requested a change and that change happened. I used what resources I had available and utilized my voice. I believe there is power in writing letters to the editor, and it's an accessible method of political activism.

Protest is an age-old tradition of political activism that has been proven to be effective, and of course, is still used today. When Americans stand up to injustice and dissent because they know the country they love can be better than this, that is a patriotic act. Suffragettes used protest to eventually win the right to vote. Civil rights activists used protests to end segregation. Change was rarely instantaneous, but the change protestors advocated for eventually did happen, and those protests have historically been cited as the catalyst for that change.

This era is ripe for dramatic social change, and the desire for this change is palpable. Political scientists have identified certain patterns and symptoms of an uprising such as economic inequality, the belief that the ruling class only serves themselves without addressing the large economic inequalities, and then there is a rise of political alternatives that were previously not feasible options. These factors work as a recipe for a political uprising.

Historically, in major revolutions, protests dramatically increase. Those who protest do so because they don't believe their voices are being heard, and so, they have little choice but to get louder and demand that they are heard. These demonstrations usually take the form of marches, petitions, boycotts, and other protests.

As resistance peaks before major revolutions, those in power must decide how to respond. If those protesting their opposition continue to be unheard, they get even louder. Once civil marches mutate into violent uprisings and those in the opposition take on more extreme action to ensure their voices are heard, the act of resistance is no longer a philosophy that rests on the fringe of society. Resistance becomes part of citizens' everyday lives.

Then, the political environment is like a ticking timebomb: seemingly anything can set it off. It doesn't have to be a large-scale coup or major event. In modern revolutions such as the Arab Spring, it began with a mundane occurrence; a fishmonger was angry with the corrupt police force. A big event, small event, doesn't matter. Something happens and then—boom! Revolution!

Now I'm not saying just because these are the symptoms of a revolution and revolutions have historically occurred in this way, that means we are on the brink of a major revolution in the United States right now. Some political scientists don't think the United States is due for a revolution; they think we're overdue. Some predicted the environment was the most apt for revolution after the financial crisis of 2007 and 2008.

That global financial crisis began in the United States. First, there was the subprime mortgage market depreciation. Then, Lehman Brothers collapsed. Then, whoops! Sorry, we broke the world financial system.

That period is when political scientists thought a revolution could occur, but it didn't, at least not in the United States. So, why didn't it happen? Well, when revolutions occur, the people also historically have had a complete distrust in the political structures and the people in power. In the years of the financial crisis, that distrust would have been warranted because a lot of people who had power over average citizens completely screwed us. Maybe people found solace in newly elected President Obama reassuring Americans that we would be ok, and people had enough trust in those in political power, we took a leap of faith instead of unleashing a full-on revolution.

Some political scientists point to the fact that there was a political revolution that had occurred; it just didn't happen in the United States. Instead, it happened in Iran which erupted into large-scale protests after their 2009 presidential election. Using the symbols of unity and hope, Iranians demanded what they viewed as a fraudulent election to be annulled.

So, perhaps a revolution did occur, it just happened elsewhere. Or maybe here in the United States, we are overdue, fully ripe, and ready for full-scale revolution. Who knows? Political science isn't perfect, and political scientists are often quite bad at making predictions. I certainly don't know. I know I was so shell shocked watching the 2016 election results roll in, I am planning on getting at least slightly inebriated before the polls close on 2020. I've learned from my mistakes and will not watch another presidential election result sober.

The fact is that revolutions are not fun. There are people who glamorize revolutions like that guy you dated in college who always wore a Che Guevara T-shirt. But the ugly truth is that to live through a revolution is to endure war, constant conflict, pain, suffering, and extreme poverty. Eventually, yes, it's true, revolutions are worth fighting for so the political system is eventually reformed. (Things are a bit of a mess now, but we, the United States, *are* the product of a revolution.) But generally, it doesn't happen until decades of political instability.

I'm not calling for a revolution in the form of a full-scale disruption and overthrowing of the entire government as we know it. I don't want to see peaceful protests erode into violence. I don't want to watch it all burn and rebuild. We're currently in a stage in this country where people are compelled to protest because it is clear that the people in power and the system in place is simply not working for the good of all.

That is why we are currently living in a fascinating time for civil discourse. The resistance is not a call for a major revolution to take over and end the United States as we know it. We're not calling to make or keep "American great again" because we understand that although there *are* great things about our country, there are many ways we are fundamentally broken. Protesting systemic failures and brokenness in our society is how we've called attention to our movement and demanded change.

There's never been a better time in United States history to get engaged in political protest than right now. All of the top five biggest protests in our country's history happened after the election of 2016. It's easy not to recognize that history is happening before our very eyes because it's happening all the time. The most well-attended protest in the United States was the 2017 Women's March held the day after Trump's inauguration, followed by the 2018 Women's March, then the 2018 March for Our Lives to protest gun violence, then the 2019 National strike in Puerto Rico, and the March for Science in 2017. Whew! Things are so wild right now, we had roughly one million scientists protesting, and you probably already forgot about it.

Protests work. You probably studied in school (or should have) the 1963 March on Washington for Jobs and Freedom. This was the march where Martin Luther King Jr. delivered his famous "I Have a Dream" speech, calling for an end to racism as he stood in front of the Lincoln Memorial in front of hundreds of thousands of people. That march is credited as being the catalyst for major social change the protestors were advocating for, including the Civil Rights Act of 1964 and the Voting Rights Act of 1965.

Throughout our history, no group has gained the societal change they were advocating for by simply asking nicely. They've had to get loud. They've had to fight. They've had to demand their voices were heard and not stop until they were. Protest is fundamentally American, as it's an exercise of our first amendment rights and a reflection of the founding of our country. The founders didn't politely proclaim, "Cheerio!" and curtsy to Great Britain as they asked for independence. They threw their Earl Grey into the harbor and launched a revolution.

I don't know what the future holds. But I know that we're living in a groundbreaking time in history. I see the evidence all around. We're hitting the streets and voicing our concerns in numbers never seen before. These are the moments our grandchildren will learn about in their history classes. They'll want to know what it was like and what we were doing.

Be able to tell them you found your voice and you made sure it was heard. You have a voice. Things may seem dire at times. But you are not powerless. Realize your power. The resistance has been fueled by women just like you who understood their power, found their voices, and demanded to be heard. You can do the same and our country will be greater for it.

CHAPTER THIRTEEN

This Is What Democracy Should Look Like

As thousands of women held their signs high above their heads and walked together onward throughout the streets of Washington, DC as part of the inaugural Women's March, a young man stood atop a tall column hovering over the crowd. He wore a T-shirt with Angela Davis's mugshot on the front and a sign that said, "Respect women of color."

He would chant into the crowd, "Show me what democracy looks like!"

The crowd would shout back, "This is what democracy looks like!"

"SHOW ME WHAT DEMOCRACY LOOKS LIKE!"

"THIS IS WHAT DEMOCRACY LOOKS LIKE!"

It was energizing to march along with a huge group of diverse women while a man supported from the sidelines. Unfortunately, that is a far cry from what democracy looks like in the United States.

2018 was a record-breaking year for women. With more women elected, the 116th Congress had the highest percentage of women of its voting members than any other time in United States history. Plus, Alexandria Ocasio-Cortez won her district's primary in a stunning upset, defeating a well-established male Democrat. She was later elected as the youngest woman ever to serve in Congress at only twenty-nine years old. Ocasio-Cortez along with newly elected women of color Rashida Tlaib, Ayanna Pressley, and Ilhan Omar (collectively known as "The Squad") shook up Congress with progressive proposals. Speaker Nancy Pelosi claimed her gavel back. It was a big year for women in politics.

But even about that record-breaking election and more women in Congress than ever before, women still make up less than a quarter of Congress. Out of 441 members in the House of Representatives, 106 are women, and out of one hundred senators, twenty-five are women. So, yes, having more women representing the people is a huge accomplishment and should be celebrated. However, less than 25 percent representation is not representative of the percentage of women in the United States.

The people we elect to represent our interests should be a reflection of the constituents they serve. The majority of people in the United States aren't white men, but the majority of members of Congress are. Non-Hispanic white people make up 61 percent of the United States, but 78 percent of Congress.

We're being governed and legislated by people who largely aren't representative of the people. When legislators do not listen to the people they represent and commit dastardly deeds for their own sake, we get laws that oppress women, people of color, and migrant communities. If 75 percent of Congress were women instead of men, do you think the rampage to defund Planned Parenthood would be as successful as it's been? If we had 78 percent of people of color in Congress, would we still be diverting money from military families to build a wall on the border of the United States and Mexico? I'm not sure, but we're a far cry from finding out with the current demographics of Congress.

If you want your interests represented, you need to elect people who reflect your interests. Having more women in Congress doesn't necessarily mean they will all progress the policy issues you care about. There are plenty of women who don't align with you politically, no matter what side of the aisle you land on.

As we've discussed, the personal *is* political, and women have intimate knowledge of women's issues. Having more women as representatives has to be more beneficial than what we have now. Aside from the huge detriment women suffer at the hands of majority male legislators, such as increased maternal mortality and reduced reproductive access, some of the comments and actions from male lawmakers will inspire you to flip the table at which you read the news. Republican State Senator Joey Hensley opposed abolishing the tax on menstrual products because he feared it would lead to out-of-control tampon buying.

This is what having a minority of women in politics looks like— you have to pay taxes on your monthly supply of menstrual products because a male lawmaker pictured you hoarding tampons like a Doomsday Prepper due to the opportunity to buy them tax-free.

Democracy should look like more women in power. To get there, we need more women to run for office, and we need to support those women to get them elected.

Find Your People

I was born, raised, and currently live in a bright red, Bible Belt, flyover state. Someone like me growing up to be a feminist and progressive political activist feels like a glitch in *The Matrix*, at times.

But once I became more involved in local politics, I learned a saying that other Democrats would say—"Blue lives here too." It's true. Sure, some Confederate flags are flying, and it's not uncommon to see someone wear a MAGA baseball hat—not out of irony. And yes, I can picture a Republican emerging from the cornfields in a hard hat like they do in their campaign ads. But there are also some incredible progressives here.

Just in my small Midwestern area, some people have made tremendous impacts on the lives of others and the fight for justice, such as Civil Rights Attorney Dan Canon. Dan served as lead counsel in the landmark Supreme Court case Obergefell v. Hodges which finally granted marriage equality in the United States. Then, some of the most active members of my local political groups are women, who I think of like my surrogate aunties; they fight for the same issues I care about while being some of the most kind, nurturing, hard-working people I've ever met. Then there are some people I consider my dearest friends who are endlessly inspirational, supportive, and just wonderful people I'm so blessed to know.

Finding this group of like-minded progressives in the same conservative area felt like discovering an exciting secret. But there are gifted, compassionate groups of people who campaign for the same issues you care about all around. If you haven't found them yet, it's time to start looking.

If you're interested in political action such as election information, campaigning, supporting candidates, and things of that nature, search for your local political group. Facebook may be a hotbed for political disinformation, but it's still a good source for meeting new progressive friends. If you live in a big city, search your city name or precinct and political party. I doubt any Republicans have made it this far into the book, so let's just go ahead and say, for example, "Democrats Precinct 4." If you live in a more rural area like I do, try searching the name of your county along with the political party.

These groups operate all over the country and are usually thrilled to have new supporters. Once you join, you'll have a lifeline to important information going into elections, opportunities to engage with candidates, and support in your community. I know being a little blue dot in a red state can be difficult sometimes, but it's a lot less difficult having a community of wonderful people who completely understand and want to make things better.

If you live in an extremely isolated area and there is not a political group that meets nearby, you can still find your community. Spend more time with like-minded friends you already have or find more through national groups that may not focus on issues specific to you geographically, but specific to the issues you care about. Like most things, you can find these groups online by simply searching using the sites you prefer.

Another way to find your community is to seek out the people who care about the same key issues you do. For example, if reducing gun violence and advocating for common-sense

gun reform legislation is a key issue for you, search for your
local Moms Demand Action chapter and attend a meeting.
If you care most about reducing racial inequality, consider
volunteering your time with local organizations run by
the Black community in your area. If you care most about
reproductive rights, consider training to be a clinic escort and
help protect women seeking abortions.

No matter where you are, you are not alone. There are
wonderful people all around you who seem overwhelmed when
you do, grieve major election losses as you do, and are fighting
the same fights you are. Political activism is easier and more
effective when you're working together. Your people are out
there. You just need to go find them.

Support Women Running for Office

One of my dear friends, one of "my people" I met through
local political action, sent me a text message recently that
she needed to ask me an important question. Then she sent
me an image of a question reminiscent of the notes young
lovebirds would pass to each other during homeroom—"Do
you like me? Check yes or no." But this note asked, "Will you
be my campaign manager?" with one "yes" box and one "no"
box below it. I couldn't pass up that kind of proposal, so I
enthusiastically responded "yes."

Campaigning is a fantastic way to support women running for
political office. Women like Alexandra Ocasio-Cortez claimed
they wore out the soles of their shoes by so much walking door
to door, canvassing voters. So much of political success is still
determined by enthusiastic boots on the ground, and there is
never a surplus of boots.

Many people are nervous to get into campaigning for a candidate at first. They're afraid voters will hang up on them, swear at them, and slam doors in their faces. Well, as someone who has knocked on their fair share of doors to share a candidate's literature and called quite a few voters to discuss a candidate's platform, let me just tell you—yes. That absolutely happens. But it doesn't happen frequently. It's just something you try not to take personally and shake off. It's not personal, it's not an attack on you. Maybe they were just watching *Fox and Friends*, and they had been just waiting for their chance to "own the libs." Just move along, realize it's not a reflection of you, and don't allow them to take any more of your time or energy. Soon enough, you won't even be fazed.

You can fit campaigning into how it best suits your lifestyle, time, and talents. Remember, you are the boss of your own time, and you should be aware of much time you want to devote to a candidate. You may love a candidate's platform and want to do all you can to get them elected, but that doesn't mean you have to devote every waking hour to contributing to their campaign. Set your boundaries and don't overextend yourself. If you have an hour to spend making calls for a candidate, there's a candidate out there who is going to be thrilled with that contribution.

The term "slacktivism" has been floated to describe the practice of advocating for political or social change using means such as social media or petitions, which involves little effort of commitment. This term is used often to insult millennials and mock their methods of activism as lazy and inefficient.

Personally? I'm a fan of "slacktivism." Some of the old school methods of campaigning are also the ones that are still most used today, especially in small, local campaigns. These methods involve strategies such as knocking on doors of voters' homes and calling them on the phone. Slacktivism critics decry millennials' efforts when they avoid these tactics. But millennials understand that other millennials do not open their doors because they listen to too many true crime podcasts and assume everyone coming unannounced is a serial killer. They don't answer phone calls received on their cell phones because they don't use them for that. If millennial campaigners have found more effective ways of reaching and engaging with voters through social media, that's just effective campaigning.

This type of environment is great for a busy mom who wants to campaign and support candidates but may not have the time or desire to stroll their kids through neighborhoods convincing voters to support their candidate. (Although if you do, your Fitbit will be *so* proud!) You can also get a list of voters to call and possibly do phone banking without leaving your kids or your home. You can campaign through social media and share why you're supporting a certain candidate. No effort is ever too small to support a campaign; any support is helpful and appreciated.

If you have more money than time to give to a campaign, you can always make a monetary donation to a candidate you support. Hosting meet-and-greets with local candidates is a perfect way for local voters to have a chance to have extra time to speak with candidates, and for candidates to raise funds and get their campaigns off the ground. To raise even more funds for the candidate you support, you can publicly share why you chose to donate to a campaign and encourage others to do the same, either independently or with a group fundraiser.

The scrutiny of female candidates on their quest to better represent their sex on the political stage is overwhelming and unwarranted. Female candidates need your support as they put themselves put there for the opportunity to better their communities and progress the issues important to them. If we want better representation, we need to elect more women to political office. If we want to elect more women to political office, we need to support their efforts. So, support women's political aspirations and help their quests to win elections become reality.

Run for Office

I pushed my toddler in the stroller and held my preschooler's hand as we entered our county courthouse the first time I ran for political office. I told them about how I wanted to make repairs at the local park and help our community. My son told everyone, "Vote for Mommy!" after I filed with the clerk's office and pushed the stroller back to our minivan.

I filed to run for a seat on a local board that managed some public properties, distributed emergency assistance for residents struggling with their utility bills, and organized community events, stuff like that. It was a real Leslie Knope position, right down to my desire to improve the parks in a small Indiana town.

On the board, there were three positions available. Two Republican incumbents were running for reelection, one new Republican, one Democrat, and yours truly. Between 60 and 65 percent of the voters I was trying to convince to vote for me voted for Trump in 2016. But I was hopeful. As far as political platforms go, mine was pretty nonpartisan. I wanted to improve the parks, be a good steward of the taxpayer's money, and help people in need. This was a small, local political office. Divisive issues like abortion access weren't being decided by the board after they finished planning the town's Easter egg hunt.

I put myself out there and made the case to voters for why I deserved a seat on the board. I was the youngest person running and the only mother. I pulled a wagon with both of my kids riding inside as I knocked on what felt like millions of doors. Some people couldn't wait to get me off their lawn, and I politely obliged, repeating my name and the office I was running for as I pulled my wagon full of kids away. Some people were thrilled at the opportunity to talk to someone about local political issues such as flooding and hazardous roads. I delivered absentee ballots to elderly voters. Once, my son demonstrated his lack of boundaries by running into a voter's house and attempting to make himself at home.

I refused to be outworked. I had limited funds, so I made my own campaign T-shirts with my vinyl cutting machine and wore it all the time. Some wonderful friends and local folks made contributions to my campaign, so I was able to purchase signs. I drove my minivan all around town and placed the signs in the most visible locations. You couldn't get a coffee, a burger, or stop at a red light around here without seeing my name. I also posted election information and campaigned on social media.

I did outwork my opponents. To my knowledge, I was the only candidate running for that office who canvassed door to door. Only one other candidate also had signs. A couple of candidates just campaigned on election day outside a polling station. I don't know of a single thing the male Republican incumbent did to campaign—no canvassing, no signs, no social media, no community engagement; he just landed on the ballot with an "R" next to his name.

A few times, I noticed subtle references to a potential loss when some people spoke to me. One of the sweet women I considered one of my Democratic Aunties once said, "Now, no matter what happens, keep coming back! We love having you involved and want to keep you around." One of my blunter friends said, "Meh. If you lose, it's ok." I didn't understand why they were even theorizing about a loss. I did not enter this race just to lose it. This wasn't a hyper-partisan race; I just wanted to repair some swings at the park. I had no intention to lose.

For months, I did everything I could to get elected. I knew I was facing a difficult battle. But it was essentially a numbers game. I examined previous election results in different precincts. I understood exactly how many votes it would take to win, so I tried to reach as many people as I possibly could to secure those votes. Each person I spoke with or made a connection, I thought *Ok. One more vote closer.* I thought about AOC walking the streets of the Bronx and Queens and making connections with voters until she wore out the soles of her shoes. This wasn't a congressional bid, and I was no AOC, but I was working hard because I knew the odds were against me too.

So. Did a young, progressive, Jewish mother win a seat previously held by a Republican in an area that has consistently voted for Republicans for decades? No. No, dear reader. I did not win. I not only lost, I got clobbered. If you recall, I ran for a board with three seats. The three Republicans running won all three. I came in dead last.

Since the results of my race were pretty...*ahem*...decisive, I realized I lost quite early in the night. I had also made friends and campaigned for other candidates, so I immediately shifted my focus to the other races. There were a couple of wins, like my good friend who won the same office I ran for in another area, a county council seat here, and a judgeship there. But most of them lost, too. I got to know brilliant women who ran hard-fought campaigns against incompetent men, and then I watched them lose. In the state, we lost all the state offices and didn't flip a single congressional district.

The sweet women who supported many campaigns and watched many local candidates come and go understood the reality of the process when she encouraged me to stick around before anyone had even voted. The harsh reality for progressive candidates in conservative areas is that, well, they lose a lot.

That same year, I did take on a couple of party-specific seats— precinct captain and convention delegate. These are, like, the most basic entry-level positions for political office. But they're important positions and actually pretty cool! (At least if you're a political nerd like me.)

Each precinct has one Republican captain and one Democrat captain. These people oversee and manage the polling location on election day and make sure Putin doesn't try to sneak in or anything like that. Precinct captains also engage in grassroots efforts to make sure registered voters get out to the polls, know where to vote, etc. Michelle Obama explained in her memoir *Becoming* that her father was a precinct captain, and she was first introduced to politics by accompanying her father on his rounds, rallying voters through the precinct.

State convention delegates contribute to that cycle's party platform, meet candidates running throughout the state, meet with specific caucuses such as the women's causes, and vote to confirm the major state candidates. In 2010, they voted to confirm Pete Buttigieg as the nominee for state treasurer, for example. (He lost too.) You've no doubt seen the National

Convention GIFs of Hillary Clinton's astonishment as balloons dropped from the ceiling. The state conventions are a lot like that, but on a smaller scale, and CNN isn't there.

The party of each state unveils a party platform each cycle, and candidates of the party throughout the state run on that platform. This can be an interesting way to influence your political party in your state because delegates have opportunities to add amendments, omissions, or changes to the platform.

The ability to influence the party platform is a great opportunity to squeeze some of your political priorities. I was able to propose changes to the party platform and include a proposal to close the gun show loophole, which allows buyers the opportunity to purchase a firearm directly in the gun show without a background check, and it was added to the official platform.

Party platforms sometimes include some proposals that read more like pipedreams, such as decriminalizing marijuana, automatic voter registration, and universal healthcare, to name a few. Here in Indiana, we just became able to buy beer on Sundays. Conservative laws and policies still reign supreme, and the political environment has not been conducive to pushing progressive ideas like universal healthcare forward. While the platform can serve as a guide for candidates, it's more about describing who the people in your party and state are as well as what you care about. While the Democratic party affirmed their commitment to LGBTQ rights, the state's GOP included language in their platform that defined marriage between a man and a woman. This was three years after marriage equality had been the law of the land. It's not always about policy proposals, it's about telling people who you are.

Both the convention delegate and the precinct captain offices have been perfect for balancing along with my role as a mother. I have an opportunity to influence the party and elections, but the demand is quite low. It's feasible to work into a typical busy mom schedule. Plus, it's fun. I like doing it. If you're basing what's happening around me politically, things look bleak based on election results and policies passed. But by being involved in the party and local politics, I can see all the incredible people doing amazing work. Instead of feeling hopeless, I feel inspired.

One thing I've found so fascinating and inspiring about these opportunities is hearing others' stories. When I went to the state convention, I got a chance to hear a beautiful, strong, Black woman speak about her congressional campaign to defeat none other than Vice President Mike Pence's brother, Greg Pence. Jeannine Lee Lake's key issues were women's rights and LGBTQ equality. She proudly supported a woman's right to choose and advocated for Medicare for All. Based in the Muncie, Indiana, area, she shared a story about how David Letterman was visiting his hometown, heard she was running against Mike Pence's brother, and immediately gave her all the money he had in his wallet.

She lost, too.

You hear stories about the campaigns of women like Representatives AOC and Ayanna Pressley because their success is so notable. Unfortunately, there are many more stories of losses like Jeannine Lee Lake's than there are stories of progressive success like Ayanna Pressley's. The harsh truth is that when you put yourself out there, you run the risk of losing. If you're trying to flip a seat, the risk is much higher. Someone's going to lose, and it might be you.

Run anyway. So what? When you put yourself out there and chase a dream you want for yourself, some degree of failure at some point is inevitable. We need to stop treating failure as a character flaw when it's just a step in the journey to success. Run a campaign you can be proud of. Work hard and stick to your convictions. If you lose, you should still put back on your campaign with pride.

We need more women to represent us, not just in the big elections that require an office in DC, but the small, local elections too. To have more women in office, we need more women to run and we need to smother these female candidates with support when they do. Running for political office usually doesn't take much more than a photo ID, residency, meeting the basic legal requirements, and a willingness to do the job. If you have that, run! If you don't want to run, campaign for women who do! If you're not willing to able to campaign, vote and do whatever you do to get these women in office.

Jeannine Lee Lake lost to Greg Pence in 2018. By 2020, she filed for a rematch. This is what women do. Things don't come easy for us. Our places aren't usually handed to us; we have to fight for them. If we lose, we get back up. Look for inspiration in the women who fight and win like Rep. Pressley. But also look for inspiration in the women who fight and keep fighting like Jeannine.

I want you and women like you to run. I don't know if you'll win. But I know you won't win if you don't run, and there are so many women out there who deserve women like you to represent them in office. So, get out there. Keep running and fighting.

CHAPTER FOURTEEN

Mom Saves the World

I was chatting with my rabbi about this book, which was still just a baby of a book at the time. I was still writing it in the fringes of the day, after my kids went to bed, when my youngest was in preschool, or honestly when they were entranced by something on Netflix. When she asked me what it was about, I told her it was about raising our children in such a way that their love overpowers evil.

This is not how I had ever described this book before. It's not how I've ever described to my agent, publisher, Uber drivers, husband, or anyone who had ever asked what the book was about. But I knew she would understand what I meant in a way that not everyone would.

In Judaism, the horrors of evil are truly never forgotten. My synagogue has a beautiful iron menorah that is carried into the chapel and lit on Yom Kippur. This menorah stands nearly as tall as I am and has six forged arms, each one representing one million Jews who perished in the Holocaust. Six million Jews.

If you've seen the classic movie *Schindler's List*, you may recall a line, "Whoever saves one life, saves the world entire." With this quote, the Jews wanted Schindler to know that by saving their lives, he has saved humanity. The origins of this quote are found in the Talmud, the central text of Jewish law and theology.

The idea is that every person holds the power of an entire world within them. Every life is capable of endless potential, and they may make tremendous contributions to humanity during their time on earth. Then, perhaps they have a child and that child may contribute to the world in extraordinary ways. The next generation does the same. Rinse and repeat until that one person is the ancestor for countless people who all did what they could to make the world a little bit better. It's like a domino effect for humanity. An entire world has been created, beginning with one person. Based on this Talmudic idea, every person carries an entire world with them. So by killing a person, a world of potential is destroyed. By saving a life that would otherwise be lost, a world of potential is saved.

That's what the Jews who were saved by Schindler were trying to convey. His actions were not limited to the 1,200 Jewish lives in front of him he saved. Because a future world exists in every person, he saved the world, or, more specifically, he saved the world 1,200 times.

This is a principle that has been used not only to illustrate the gravity of what every single life represents and the preciousness of each life, but also to teach that bystanders have a moral obligation to stand up and defend lives in danger. It's also been used to promote peace and pacifism.

This belief is what makes bringing out a menorah to represent the six million Jews who perished in the Holocaust in front of a congregation of Jews who live today so meaningful. Worlds were destroyed. Worlds were saved. We see and remember evidence of both.

So, when I talk about the presence of evil to my rabbi, it feels natural. She doesn't flinch. She doesn't respond, "Ugh, Farrah, you're such a downer today." Evil has always been and continues to be a constant reality. We remember the evil that destroyed worlds before. We're confronted with the evil that destroys worlds today, such as the tragedy occurring in 2018 when a man, emboldened by hate, entered a Pittsburgh synagogue with an AR-15 and committed the deadliest attack on the Jewish community in the United States to date. We understand the moral obligation that we have to do what we can to, well, save the world.

Those who maintain the memories of those who perished in the Holocaust don't just educate others about the genocide itself or simply memorialize the victims. They educate others about what happened before that point to ensure it doesn't happen again. Director of the US Holocaust Memorial Museum Sara Bloomfield said in an interview with the *Washington Post*, "Nazis didn't fall out of the sky in January 1933." One chilling history lesson from the museum is the statement, "The Holocaust did not begin with killing; it began with words."

So, it's disturbing when echoes of those words are heard today as neo-Nazi Richard Spencer rallies a force of angry people with the principle that this country belongs to white people and they are facing a "conquer or die" type of a decision that is reminiscent of the words that predated the Holocaust and influenced Adolf Hitler's philosophy that there was a racial struggle for survival. We have a sexual predator in the White House who regularly flirts with fascism and passes cruel, xenophobic policies. People have become so far removed and desensitized to the suffering of others, they choose to send thoughts and prayers with a praying hand emoji instead of enacting policy change that would actually save lives.

Things are bad.

So, as I talk about this book to my rabbi and explain that I want to empower mothers to overthrow evil with the way they raise their children, she nods as if this is a reasonable concept that makes total sense. As I'm speaking with her, I'm trying to piece together these abstract ideas of a way to transform evil into love and create a more hopeful future. But I'm just positive I sound like someone on *Drunk History* because it's not making any sense.

But, my rabbi responded, "Aha! Sweetening the evil."

She recommended a book including this concept that is an analysis of several different rabbis' theories on the story of Jacob's Ladder in Genesis. Now, dear reader, if you are not Jewish or religious, do not despair. These teachings have roots in Jewish mysticism, also known as Kabbalah, which was trendy among celebrities in the early 2000s. You do not have to be Jewish, religious, or Madonna to understand or find meaning in this.

An ancient female rabbi repeated a principle she learned from Hasidism, "find the root of love in evil to sweeten evil and turn it into love." Hundreds of years later, Jewish scholars have theorized on this quote and the context behind it which eventually brought them to the idea of the "evil other."

The other is something that has come up in Shakespearean works and the study of ethics. The other is just someone different in some way than yourself or the status quo. "Othering" is the concept of labeling and defining a person as someone on the fringes of society. It's historically been used in racism and genocide. Structural othering is used when people are labeled "illegal immigrants," for example. So this is something that has happened for hundreds and years and continues to exist.

The "evil other" in this ancient context is someone who we view as a hateful person unlike ourselves. But what those who study and theorize about the texts say is that the evil other may be a reflection of ourselves. The otherness is just an illusion. To destroy our capacity for evil, we must show love toward what we hate in the so-called evil other. Under this philosophy, we can extinguish evil by embracing what was never really other.

Whoa. Heavy, right? Ok, stay with me.

So, in Judaism, the concepts of enemies and evilness come up a lot because as long as they have been Jews, there have been people trying to kill us. Nearly every Jewish holiday follows a "They tried to kill us, they failed, let's eat" formula. There's evil out there in the world. People want to defeat evil, but without sacrificing what makes them good. This can be really hard. Think about a time you witnessed evil and how it affected you. How about when we watched the Unite the Right rally unfold? Neo-Nazis marched through the streets of Charlottesville, Virginia, wearing swastikas and shouted, "you will not replace us!" Resistor Heather Heyer, who came to stand up to bigotry and hatred, was killed. Then, when asked for comment, Donald Trump couldn't even point to which side were the bad guys. (Hint: It's the Nazis. The Nazis are always the bad guys. There was a whole war about this. One of the big ones.)

That felt like witnessing something evil. When I watched news coverage of young men holding a tiki torch in one hand and doing a Sieg Heil salute with the other, it felt like evil. Then, that unleashed a whole host of emotions in myself that I don't like—sadness, despair, fear, anger, resentment.

The thought behind "sweetening the evil" is that if you have a pure heart and a focused mind, you may get to what is still good in the root of the evildoer and pull them toward lightness and raise it to the good. Behind this philosophy is the idea that evil can be rectified and made good.

But it's a tall order, right? How are you supposed to get to the root of evil? Are you supposed to approach Richard Spencer as he's leading a parade of Nazis and ask, "Ok, Rich, let's get to the root of the problem. What was your childhood like? Were you bullied? When did things go awry?" Even if we have the will to turn those who exude hatred into those who radiate love, even by this theory, it only works if there is still goodness in the person promoting evil.

It's not the best plan to seek out bigots, sexists, and xenophobes because you hate what they represent and you want to psychoanalyze the root of their evilness so you can transform them to good. You put yourself in potential danger. It may be possible to convert someone, but it's not probable. There are too many factors outside of your control.

However, there are factors within your control and the power you have to accomplish the same goal of combating misogyny, bigotry, and inequality in the pursuit of a more just, kind world. To embrace the evil that was never really other, we have to examine how we contribute to what we hate. This looks like practicing anti-racism and feminism. That is well within our control. To defeat sexism and bigotry, we have to look within ourselves and accept that we're perennial works in progress.

In practicing activism, we have to be fiercely compassionate. We have to, by default, show others the empathy and compassion they deserve. This love should be extended to our partners, our communities, our fellow mothers, our children, and ourselves.

As activists, we can't allow ourselves to drag down as we work to combat the evils and injustices of the world until that evil also becomes a part of us. We have to stay hopeful and keep focused on the fight for a better future. It's what we and our children deserve.

As mothers, we have an enormous responsibility. Just as that Talmudic reference in *Schindler's List* embodies, each life signifies an entire world. We have created a new life and our children have entire worlds of potentials within them. How we raise them and what we teach them is what will shape their world.

People like to ask silly rhetorical questions about time traveling and how having the opportunity to make minor, seemingly insignificant actions in the past would make huge impacts. But people rarely ask what actions you could take now to make an impact on the future.

No one needs to theorize about what actions they would do to stop the Nazis in the 1930s or how they would support civil rights in the 1960s. Whatever you *would* do is what you're doing right now. History is happening. Your grandchildren are going to ask you what you did in these moments. What do you want to be proud to tell them?

When you're seemingly surrounded by injustice, it can feel overwhelming and you may feel like you don't have enough power to fight it. But you already are. You see the future of humanity all the time as you raise and love your children.

Martin Luther King Jr. said, "the arc of the moral universe is long, but it bends toward justice." Dr. King didn't live to see the justice he sought in his lifetime, but it was his activism that sent his goals to fruition. Progress can be slow, and we still live in a world full of injustice. But thanks largely to the activism of the past, we've also experienced groundbreaking strides toward a more righteous world.

The arc of the moral universe doesn't bend on its own; we must put in the work in the pursuit of future justice. You have the power to bend the arc by raising your kids to resist bigotry, misogyny, and hatred. By teaching our children love, they will overpower evil. Mothering is one of the most influential acts of activism as the future of humanity lies in our children. If you want to save the world, you can start with the way you raise the future.

RESOURCES

As you continue your journey into activism, here are some further resources you may find helpful.

Further Reading

These are fantastic books I personally love which dive further into some of the concepts I discussed in *Raising the Resistance: A Mother's Guide to Practical Activism.*

+ *Women, Race, and Class* by Angela Davis

> Angela Davis is brilliant feminist icon, and in this book, you will gain a necessary history of modern feminist movements so you can learn from previous shortcomings and find inspiration in the past.

+ *Feminism is For Everybody* by bell hooks

> bell hooks is another feminist icon, and her work is essential reading for further understanding of the intersection of feminism, race, and class. We have so much to learn from her wisdom.

+ *How to Be an Antiracist* by Ibram X. Kendi

> Dr. Kendi is the pioneer of anti-racism, and this book is like taking a master class. MUST read.

+ *Sister Outsider* by Audre Lorde

> This is a great one if you're ready to dive a little deeper into feminism and get lost in the beauty of Lorde's words. You'll emerge refreshed and energized to do some serious work toward social justice.

+ *So You Want to Talk About Race* by Ijeoma Oluo

> This is essential reading for thoroughly understanding modern civil rights movements and how you should find your own place in combating white supremacy.

+ *We Are Not Here to Be Bystanders: A Memoir of Love and Resistance* by Linda Sarsour

> Linda is a tireless crusader for civil rights, and I am confident she will be remembered as one of the greatest activists of our resistance for decades to come. Her memoir captures her poignancy and passion beautifully.

+ *Fight Like a Mother* by Shannon Watts

> Like me, Shannon was a stay-at-home mom in the Hoosier state. But then she built a grassroots movement that turned into the NRA's worst nightmare. This is a must-read for organizer moms.

+ *Shrill* by Lindy West

> Reading *Shrill* is like having margaritas with your best friend. You won't want to put this one down.

Organizations

Here are some of my favorite organizations. Many of these groups have chapters throughout the United States (and sometimes the world!), so please find a chapter near you.

+ Black Lives Matter

It's so much more than a hashtag, Black Lives Matter defines one of the most crucial civil rights movements in our time. Find time to locate your local chapter, read through their platform and resources, and support your local movement.

+ Moms Demand Action

The most influential gun safety and control group in the United States, plus moms are running the show.

+ Mom Hugs

This is another great LGBTQ+ organization, this time built and supported by moms. I love the spirit behind this.

+ RAICES

Immigration is an extremely important civil rights issue as concentration camps currently hold migrants in horrific conditions on American soil. This organization is working hard for migrant families across the country. Be sure to locate your local refugee groups as well to support.

+ Sisters of Perpetual Indulgence

I love this LGBTQ+ charity. They do fantastic work throughout the country, but also are a wonderful source for LGBTQ+ outreach.

+ Planned Parenthood Action

> This arm of Planned Parenthood will keep you tuned into
> the latest news related to reproductive justice, so you can
> help where you're most needed.

Beyond that, find organizations tuned into the key issues you
care about most!

Diving further into activism and putting in the work makes
a real difference and will help make our resistance successful
for the next generation. I'm proud of you. Keep learning, keep
growing, keep going!

ACKNOWLEDGMENTS

I'm grateful to my former self for channeling the chutzpah I had into fulfilling my lifelong dream of writing a book. But of course, this was not done alone, and I was blessed with the best people sustaining me with their wisdom and loving support.

To my husband, Patrick—thank you for loving a woman who evolved from the one you married. You have pushed me to accomplish more than I ever thought possible, and there's no one I would rather share my dreams and life with more than you. I love you.

To my beautiful children, Daniel and Penelope—I never knew how much love my heart could hold until I held you in my arms. Thank you for being understanding beyond your years as Mommy couldn't always play as the deadline loomed. You amaze me with your sweet souls and spirits. I will forever fight for a world that better reflects the kindness you both exhibit every day. I love you forever.

To my parents—whether I was coloring my hair pink as a teenager or causing a ruckus as an adult, you've always met me with unconditional love and support. I'm forever grateful for the lessons you've taught and the values you instilled which made me into the woman I am today. I love, respect, and admire you both so much.

To my dearest family and friends—thank you for always being there. I'll never forget those of you who believed in me from the very beginning, before the book was born, and encouraged me to push forward. From my mom and mother-in-law providing countless hours of childcare to my best of friends celebrating small wins, you all made this possible, and I can't thank you enough.

To my fierce agent, Alice Speilburg—you have been an absolute champion for this book and made it into what it became. Your brilliant contributions were vital to the end product. I can't imagine navigating the process of publishing a debut book without your expertise, humor, kindness, and patience. Thank you for believing in this project from the beginning and carrying that enthusiasm to publication.

To my acquiring editor, Brenda Knight, editors Yaddyra Peralta and Robin Miller, and the team at Mango—thank you all sincerely for your insight, creativity, and guidance. Your enthusiasm from the beginning thrilled me to be with Mango, and I'm still so grateful for the opportunity.

Finally, to all the readers—thank you for caring so deeply and investing in the idea that we can do better. I have faith that with your talents, compassion, and relentless pursuit of doing what is right, we will leave a more just world for our children.

ABOUT THE AUTHOR

Farrah Alexander is a writer whose work focuses on feminism, parenting, social justice, politics, and current events. Her work has been featured in *Huffington Post*, *BUST*, and *Scary Mommy*. Her commentary has been discussed in *Scientific American, Buzzfeed, Refinery 29, Yahoo, Hello Giggles, Woke Sloth, Cosmopolitan, Elle, Perez Hilton, Daily Mail, BBC*, and others.

Raising the Resistance: A Mother's Guide to Practical Activism is her debut book. She is a member of the Everytown Author's Council, which was designed to "harness the power of the literary community to amplify the gun safety movement." She is a Jeremiah Fellow with Bend the Arc: A Jewish Partnership for Justice, along with a cohort of young, progressive Jews dedicated to fighting white supremacy, anti-Semitism, and injustice. She holds a Bachelor of Arts in Political Science from Indiana University.

She lives outside Louisville, Kentucky, with her husband, son, and daughter.

Mango Publishing, established in 2014, publishes an eclectic list of books by diverse authors—both new and established voices—on topics ranging from business, personal growth, women's empowerment, LGBTQ studies, health, and spirituality to history, popular culture, time management, decluttering, lifestyle, mental wellness, aging, and sustainable living. We were recently named 2019 *and* 2020's #1 fastest growing independent publisher by *Publishers Weekly*. Our success is driven by our main goal, which is to publish high quality books that will entertain readers as well as make a positive difference in their lives.

Our readers are our most important resource; we value your input, suggestions, and ideas. We'd love to hear from you—after all, we are publishing books for you!

Please stay in touch with us and follow us at:

Facebook: Mango Publishing
Twitter: @MangoPublishing
Instagram: @MangoPublishing
LinkedIn: Mango Publishing
Pinterest: Mango Publishing

Sign up for our newsletter at www.mangopublishinggroup.com and receive a free book!

Join us on Mango's journey to reinvent publishing, one book at a time.

CPSIA information can be obtained
at www.ICGtesting.com
Printed in the USA
JSHW011433090920
7733JS00002B/2